ENGLAND THROUGH THE AGES

A CONCISE GUIDE

By

Martin Miller-Yianni

Royal Arms of England

COPYRIGHT AND ACKNOWLEDGEMENTS

Publisher: Martin Miller-Yianni, Yambol, Bulgaria

First Printed Edition 2024

ISBN: 978-619-7742-31-2 (paperback)

ISBN: 978-619-7742-32-9 (ePub)

A CIP catalogue record for this book is available from:

The National Register of Published Books in Bulgaria

bulevard 'Vasil Levski' 88,

1504 Sofia,

Bulgaria

Cover Photograph (Stonehenge, Wiltshire)

by Mitch Hodge from Unsplash.com

CONTENTS

INTRODUCTION

"England Through the Ages: A Concise Guide" serves as a valuable reference for students, inquisitive travellers, and those intrigued by the captivating history of England. This book is part of a series of books about the history of various countries. All the books have well-organised structures and clear presentations that facilitate easy navigation through various historical periods, allowing readers to swiftly locate specific information.

From the ancient civilisations of England to contemporary developments, this book comprehensively covers essential facets of England's history. It enables readers to grasp the historical context and cultural heritage of the region. The concise format makes it an ideal choice for those seeking a quick reference or an introduction to England's past.

Presented in a readable and accessible British English style, the book offers a comprehensive overview without compromising on accuracy or depth. This quality makes it an excellent resource for gaining knowledge about England's diverse historical foundations.

It's worth noting that some chapters may recap and explain important events as in previous chapters. Such recapitulations are inevitable, as era transitions often share events and important figures, reinforcing the interconnectedness of England's history. They serve as valuable reminders, aiding in comprehending the broader historical narrative.

Whether you aim to refresh your knowledge of a specific historical era or develop a general understanding of England's past, this book delivers reliable information and serves as an invaluable guide. It immerses readers in the triumphs, challenges, and cultural metamorphoses that have contributed to England's identity, offering a fascinating journey through time.

This book stands as an engaging and informative read that provides a succinct yet comprehensive look at England's history. It remains an exceptional resource for anyone eager to explore the fascinating story of this region and gain a deeper appreciation for its rich cultural heritage.

The Flag of England

The English flag boasts a distinctive and impactful design that encapsulates the essence of the nation's rich history and cultural heritage. It features a red cross on a white background. This design holds deep historical and cultural significance for England, representing key elements of its identity.

The red cross on a white background symbolises various aspects of England's history. The red cross, known as the St. George's Cross, is associated with Saint George, the patron saint of England. The white background signifies purity and has been a prominent element in England's heraldic traditions.

Officially adopted as the flag of England, the St. George's Cross is a source of immense pride for the English people. Its symbolism goes beyond aesthetics, serving as a visual representation of England's enduring spirit, cultural heritage, and the values that have shaped the nation throughout its history. The flag, with its evocative design and historical resonance, stands as a powerful emblem of English unity and identity.

The St. George's Cross has a longstanding historical connection, and its use has evolved over the centuries, making it a symbol that resonates with England's past and present. The flag serves as a powerful reminder of the nation's journey and contributions to the world, standing as a testament to English pride and heritage.

The Location of England

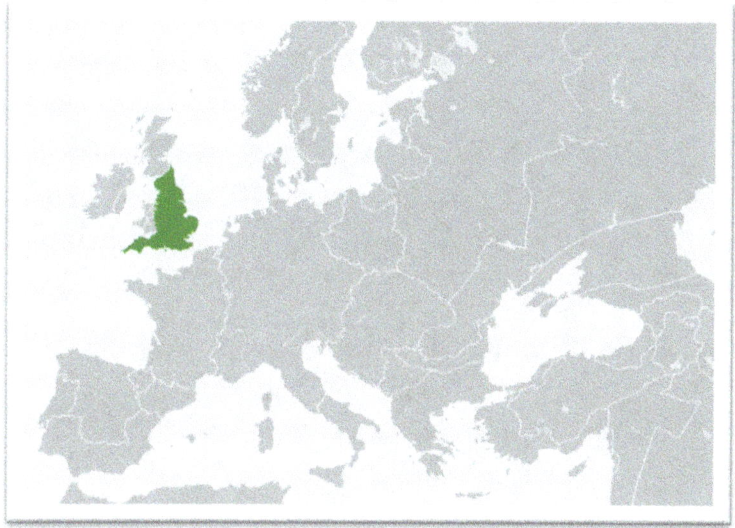

England, spanning approximately 130,279 square kilometres, occupies a strategic location at the crossroads of history and cultural influences, situated in the British Isles. The country's diverse geography encompasses various features, including picturesque landscapes like the Pennines and the Lake District, expansive plains, and a notable coastline along the North Sea, the English Channel, and the Irish Sea.

The extensive coastline, bordered by the North Sea to the east, the English Channel to the south, and the Irish Sea to the west, has significantly influenced England's cultural and economic activities throughout history.

England shares its borders with several countries, fostering historical connections and cultural exchanges. It is bordered by Scotland to the north and Wales to the west. These geographical connections have played a vital role in shaping England's history and contributing to its cultural diversity.

The country is traversed by numerous rivers, including the Thames and the Severn, contributing to its varied landscapes and supporting agricultural activities. The climate in England varies from maritime along the coastal areas to more temperate in the interior and southern regions.

CHAPTER 1 - PREHISTORIC ENGLAND

UP TO 43 A.D.

Ancient England has been a land of mystery and allure since long before recorded history. For nearly one million years, Homo sapiens have been living and adapting within the British Isles. This period is known as the Paleolithic era, and these ancient people faced many challenges. Despite the presence of undulating hills and lush valleys, they were constantly on the move in search of sustenance.

The Old Stone Age was a time of great achievement for the people of Britain. They had the creativity and skill to create tools from flint and stone, and they used them to forge an existence in an unforgiving environment. This was a time of unity between people and nature, as they learned to work with the seasons and the land to create a sustainable lifestyle. The sound of flint on flint and the echoing of the hand axe was a reminder of how far humanity had come. It was an indication of their triumph over the wilds of England and a symbol of their mastery over nature. This was a time of resilience, adaptation and the pursuit of sustenance, a story that still resonates through the years.

Now, let the Mesolithic era unfold. In approximately 6500 B.C., the rising sea levels permanently separated Britain from the continent. During this time, the population, comprising exclusively of anatomically modern humans, displayed signs of advancing societal complexity. There is evidence suggesting that these inhabitants engaged in innovative environmental manipulation, including the selective burning of prevalent woodlands to establish clearings for herds to assemble, subsequently facilitating hunting activities. The primary hunting tools at this juncture were simple projectile weapons such as javelins and possibly slings. It is noteworthy that the knowledge of the bow and arrow in Western Europe dates back to at least 9000 B.C. Concurrently, the climate continued to warm, likely contributing to a population increase during this period.

In the Middle Stone Age, cultural togetherness became the prevailing theme. Improved tools and semi-permanent abodes painted a vibrant picture of human resilience and progression against the ever-shifting landscapes of ancient England.

The Neolithic era, also known as the New Stone Age, commenced around 4000 B.C. with the introduction of farming, a practice believed to have originated from the Middle East. The exact cause of this shift remains uncertain, whether it resulted from a significant migration of people, the adoption of foreign practices by the indigenous population, or a combination of both. This period marked a transition to a more settled lifestyle. Notably, collective tombs, such as chambered cairns and long barrows, were constructed for the deceased.

As the era progressed, monumental stone alignments like Stonehenge emerged, displaying a fascination with celestial alignments and planets. Flint technology during this time yielded both highly artistic pieces and practical tools. To create fields and pastures, there was a notable increase in woodland clearance. The Sweet Track in the Somerset Levels, dated to the winter of 3807–3806 B.C. through dendrochronology, stands as one of the oldest timber trackways in Northern Europe, believed to have had primarily religious significance. Additionally, archaeological findings in North Yorkshire suggest the production of salt during the Neolithic times.

Stonehenge c.3000-2500 B.C.

The Neolithic era in England unfolded as a flux of agricultural innovation, cultural expression, and communal resilience, etching indelible marks on the canvas of our shared human history.

Now, into the Bronze Age cast its shimmering glow across the historical landscape from 2500 B.C. to 800 B.C. This pivotal juncture witnessed the transformative embrace of bronze – a metal alloy of copper and tin – revolutionising the crafting of tools and weapons, ushering in an era of technological advancement.

Early Bronze Age Dagger

Around 2400 B.C., a significant chapter unfolded with the arrival of the Beaker People, not only bringing coveted bronze tools but also introducing novel burial practices. Their presence resonated with an amalgamation of cultural exchange and technological prowess, leaving an indelible mark on the evolving narrative of this age.

Witness the mastery of casting techniques becoming a hallmark of the Bronze Age, propelling craftsmanship to unprecedented heights. This technological leap not only enhanced the efficiency of tools and weaponry but also laid the foundation for a flourishing trade network. The landscape witnessed the glint of bronze tools in the hands of craftsmen, the echoes of trade routes crisscrossing the land, and the imposing stature of hill forts against the skyline, defining an era that sculpted the contours of ancient England.

The Iron Age arrived and cast its enduring shadow from approximately 800 B.C. to 43 CE, standing as a crucial era witnessing a profound transformation with the emergence of iron tools. This era signifies a technological leap and heightened social complexity.

During this era, the Celts emerged as the dominant force combined with a mixture of tribes and chiefdoms across the British Isles. As the clang of iron replaced the resonance of bronze, witness a metamorphosis in the landscape marked by the construction of imposing hill forts and the expansion of trade connections with continental Europe.

The advent of iron tools represented more than a mere shift in metallurgy; it symbolised a leap forward in technological prowess. The Celts, with their mastery of ironworking, wielded tools and weapons surpassing their predecessors in both efficiency and durability. This transition laid the groundwork for a society embracing innovation and adaptability.

Hillforts, once a hallmark of the Bronze Age, continued to punctuate the landscape, reflecting an evolved form of social organisation. Strategically positioned and fortified, these strongholds served as symbols of power and practical defences against external threats. The Iron Age communities embraced a more intricate social fabric, characterised by a hierarchy of leadership and an organised system of governance.

Cadbury Castle a Bronze/Iron Age Hillfort

Trade connections flourished during this period, extending beyond the island's borders to continental Europe. The Celts engaged in vibrant exchanges of goods, ideas, and cultural practices, enriching the culture of both regions. The echoes of trade caravans and iron implements resonated across the landscape, weaving a narrative of interconnectedness and cultural dynamism.

The conventional beginning of the Iron Age is placed around 800 B.C., during which the Celtic Britons were settled in England. The majority of the population consisted of Celtic people, alongside smaller ethnic groups in Great Britain. This demographic composition persisted from the British Iron Age into the Middle Ages until it was eventually supplanted by the Germanic Anglo-Saxons. Over time, the Celtic Britons diversified into distinct ethnic groups such as the Welsh, Cornish, and Breton, though they remained connected through language, religion, and culture, primarily speaking the Brittonic language, a Celtic precursor to modern Brittonic languages.

Maiden Castle Hillfort in Dorset

During this period, the Atlantic system effectively collapsed, but England maintained connections with France across the channel as the Hallstatt culture became widespread. The continuity of this culture suggests minimal population movement, with only one known Hallstatt burial in Britain. Burial practices changed, with a shift towards archaeologically invisible methods such as excarnation. Hillforts, known since the Late Bronze Age, proliferated between 600 and 400 B.C., especially in the South. After 400 B.C., new forts were seldom built, and many ceased regular habitations, indicating some regional centralisation.

Contact with the continent persisted, albeit less than in the Bronze Age. Goods continued to flow to England, with a potential interruption around 350 to 150 B.C. Two known invasions occurred during this period: around 300 B.C., the Gaulish Parisii tribe took control of East Yorkshire, establishing the distinctive Arras culture, and from approximately 150–100 B.C., groups of Belgae began to dominate significant parts of the South.

IMPORTANT PEOPLE AND PLACES DURING THIS PERIOD

PEOPLE:

Beaker People (2400 B.C.): Migrants of the Bronze Age, influencing both culture and burial practices.

Celts (800 B.C. - 43 A.D.): The Celts were known for their intricate metalwork, polytheistic religious practices, and formidable warrior culture.

PLACES:

Stonehenge (3100 B.C. - 1600 B.C.): A Neolithic monument whose purpose, be it astronomical or religious, remains shrouded in mystery.

Skara Brae (3100 B.C. - 2500 B.C.): A well-preserved Neolithic village in Orkney, unveiling glimpses of ancient life.

Maiden Castle (600 B.C. - 43 A.D.): An Iron Age hill fort in Dorset, standing as a testament to ancient defensive strategies.

CHAPTER 2 - ROMAN ENGLAND

43 – 410 A.D.

As the celestial dance of time gracefully unfurled, a truly distinctive chapter unwound its pages, ushering in the resplendent times of Roman England, an illustrious span extending from 43 to 410 A.D. During this extraordinary period, the verdant landscapes of England found themselves cradled within the formidable embrace of the mighty Roman Empire—a chapter marked not just by conquest and assimilation but by the enduring legacy that still stands the trials of time in England.

In the grand plethora of history, the monumental year 43 A.D. stands as a crucible when the shores of England bore witness to the majestic arrival of Roman legions under the august command of Emperor Claudius. Despite the steadfast resistance put forth by indigenous tribes, the indomitable Roman war machine triumphed, resolutely establishing Roman dominion by 47 A.D., unfurling the banner of Roman England with unparalleled grandeur.

The Romans, revered across antiquity for their unparalleled military prowess, brought forth not only the sheer might of their legions but also an intricately woven administrative system that would indelibly shape the destiny of this lush region. Sprawling urban centres, such as the venerable Londinium, now the pulsating heart of modern-day London, emerged as bustling hubs of commerce and governance, intricately connected by an expanse of well-constructed roads, with the illustrious Watling Street etching its path into the very fabric of the landscape.

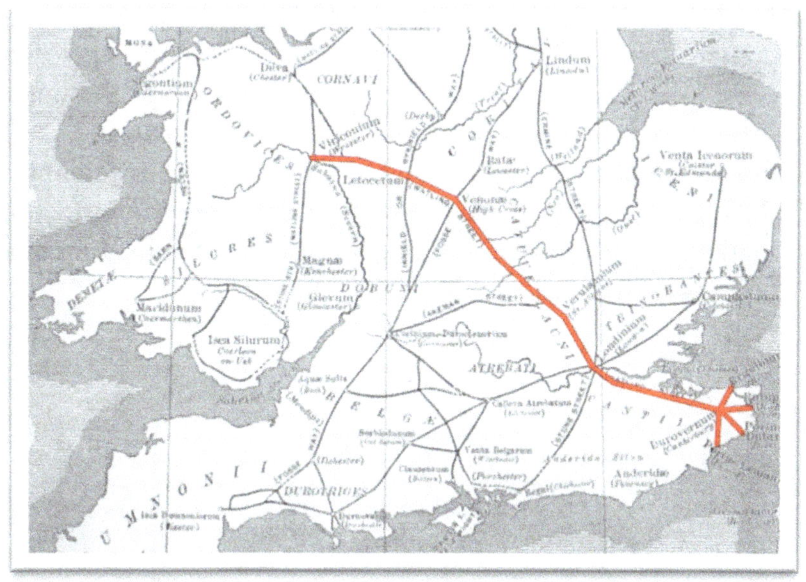

Watling Street Route

The far-reaching influence of Roman culture pervaded every facet of English life that showcased the seamless fusion between Roman refinement and the rich indigenous traditions. Local customs, linguistic expressions, and architectural wonders bore the unmistakable imprint of Roman sophistication. Villas, adorned with intricate mosaic floors, became exquisite expressions of this harmonious blend, while elaborate bathhouses stood as living testaments to the cultural symbiosis that defined the era. The resonance of Latin in everyday discourse not only echoed through bustling marketplaces but also lingered in the cadence of the English language, leaving an indelible mark on linguistic landscapes for generations to come.

A crowning jewel in the diadem of Roman engineering and military prowess was the majestic Hadrian's Wall, a colossus erected between the years 122 A.D. and 128 A.D. Stretching regally across the northern reaches of England, this monumental fortification stood as a resplendent testament to the might of Roman England—a colossal defensive bulwark that marked the very extremities of the sprawling Roman Empire, echoing with the silent whispers of centuries past.

Hadrian's Wall

While the Roman military played a pivotal role in safeguarding the realms of England, the vicissitudes faced by the Roman Empire led to a gradual diminution of the garrison. The poignant withdrawal of Roman legions in 410 A.D. marked the melancholic denouement of Roman England, drawing the curtain on an extraordinary chapter in history—an evanescent but epochal era that left an indelible mark on the collective consciousness.

Yet, despite the relatively fleeting nature of its temporal tenure, the legacy of Roman rule endured, casting its imprimatur in the heart of English society. The echo of Roman governance, the enduring infrastructure, and the rich amalgamation of cultural hues painted on this historical canvas manifested a cultural legacy that transcended time. The architectural wonders of the Romans, including awe-inspiring amphitheatres and resplendent baths, persisted as silent witnesses to a bygone era—an era when England, with open arms, embraced the grandeur of the Roman Empire.

Roman Baths in Bath

Embarking on an exploration of the remnants of Roman England invites contemplation on a bygone era when the land, with open arms, embraced the grandeur of the Roman Empire. Hadrian's Wall, standing stoically as a silent witness, echoes the triumphant conquests and monumental constructions that defined this captivating period, inviting modern minds to journey through the corridors of time and immerse themselves in the grandeur of a civilisation that once graced these ancient lands.

IMPORTANT PEOPLE, PLACES AND EVENTS DURING THIS PERIOD

PEOPLE:

Emperor Claudius (10 B.C. – 54 A.D.): Led the Roman invasion of Britain in 43 A.D., marking the beginning of Roman rule.

Emperor Hadrian (76 A.D. – 138 A.D.): Ordered the construction of Hadrian's Wall between 122 and 128 A.D.

Boudica (d. 60/61 A.D.): Queen of the Iceni tribe, led a famous uprising against Roman rule in 60/61 A.D.

Agricola (40 A.D. – 93 A.D.): Roman governor of Britain from 77 to 85 A.D., known for his military campaigns and infrastructure development.

Constantine the Great (272 – 337 A.D.): Born in Roman Britain, later became the Roman Emperor and played a crucial role in the Christianisation of the empire.

PLACES:

Londinium (London): The Roman provincial capital, established as a major city with forums, temples, and baths.

Hadrian's Wall: A defensive fortification built across northern England, spanning approximately 73 miles.

Colchester (Camulodunum): One of the earliest Roman settlements in Britain, Colchester became the first Roman capital.

Bath (Aquae Sulis): Known for its Roman-built baths and temple complex, showcasing Roman urban planning.

Eboracum (York): An important Roman city with a fortress, serving as a strategic military and administrative centre.

EVENTS:

Roman Invasion (43 A.D.): Emperor Claudius led the Roman legions in the successful invasion of Britain, initiating Roman rule.

Boudiccan Revolt (60/61 A.D.): Boudica, angered by Roman mistreatment, led a rebellion resulting in the destruction of several Roman settlements.

Construction of Hadrian's Wall (122–128 A.D.): Emperor Hadrian ordered the building of the iconic defensive barrier in northern Britain.

Romanisation and Urbanisation: The establishment of Roman cities, roads, and infrastructure led to the Romanisation of Britain.

Council of Carthage (314 A.D.): The Council of Carthage, with British bishops in attendance, played a role in early Christian church developments in Britain.

Roman Withdrawal (410 A.D.): The Roman legions withdrew from Britain in 410 A.D. due to pressing issues within the Roman Empire.

CHAPTER 3 - ANGLO-SAXON AND VIKING ERA

410-1066 A.D.

The passage from the Roman withdrawal in 410 A.D. to the time-defining Norman Conquest in 1066 unfolded as a watershed moment in the countless years of British history, an era intricately woven with the threads of both the Anglo-Saxon and Viking times. With the graceful exit of the Roman legions, the Anglo-Saxons, comprising formidable Germanic tribes such as the Angles, Saxons, and Jutes, surged forth, filling the void left by the departing Romans and forging a mosaic of kingdoms that included Wessex, Mercia, Northumbria, and East Anglia.

In the stratified layers of Anglo-Saxon society, regal figures like Æthelberht of Kent, Æthelstan, and the illustrious Alfred the Great stood resolute atop the hierarchical pyramid. Alfred, in particular, etched his name in history defending England against relentless Viking raids, earning the sobriquet "the Great" for his military prowess, legal reforms, and fervent commitment to learning. The Viking invasions, spanning the 8th to the 11th centuries, with their iconic longships carving through tumultuous waves, added a discordant note to the historical archives.

Amidst the challenges posed by the Viking incursions, influential figures such as Dunstan, Archbishop of Canterbury, and Æthelstan, the first King of England, emerged as stalwart custodians of Anglo-Saxon heritage. The Danelaw, a region firmly under Viking control, introduced Norse laws and customs, casting its own formidable shadow over the Anglo-

Saxon landscape. The climactic Battle of Hastings in 1066, where William the Conqueror triumphed, marked the poignant conclusion of the Anglo-Saxon era, unravelling established foundations and introducing new motifs of governance, culture, and language.

Æthelstan, The First King of England

Certain key locations played pivotal roles during this transformative era. Wessex, with its capital at the venerable Winchester, stood as a bulwark against Viking invasions, producing notable rulers such as Alfred the Great. Canterbury, an ecclesiastical hub, bore witness to Augustine's mission, a pivotal moment in the conversion of the Anglo-Saxons. The venerable Jarrow and Wearmouth Monasteries, bastions of learning, became the nurturing grounds for luminaries such as the venerable Bede.

The Viking Age, stretching from the late 8th to the early 11th centuries, brought forth relentless raids, daring trading ventures, and enduring settlements. The ominous Lindisfarne raid in 793 set the tone for brutal incursions, ultimately leading to the establishment of the Danelaw. Alfred the Great's staunch defence, culminating in the pivotal Battle of Edington, marked a transformative turning point in the struggle against Viking onslaught.

The enduring legacy of the Viking Age manifested in profound linguistic and cultural integration. Old Norse words seamlessly wove into the fabric of the English language, and the indelible imprint of Viking influence persisted in the nomenclature of places within the Danelaw. Settlements and cultural amalgamation fostered a harmonious blending of Norse and Anglo-Saxon traditions, laying the groundwork for the eventual emergence of a unified England.

Key figures from the Viking Age, including the legendary Ragnar Lothbrok, the valiant Alfred the Great, the influential Canute the Great, and the formidable Harald Hardrada, left an indelible mark on the historical landscape. Noteworthy locations such as the symbolic Lindisfarne, the bustling trading and settlement centre of Jorvik (York), and pivotal events like the Battle of Edington and the occupation by the Viking Great Army played pivotal roles in shaping the Danelaw and the broader course of history.

Harald Hardrada in Kirkwall Cathedral

As the Viking Age gracefully paved the way for the transformative Norman Conquest, England stood at the threshold of a new era, embracing diverse influences and shaping its destiny through a constant process of evolution. The echoes of the Anglo-Saxon past and the transformative Viking Age resonated through the corridors of time, leaving an enduring and profound mark on the rich maze of England's history.

IMPORTANT PEOPLE, PLACES AND EVENTS DURING THIS PERIOD

PEOPLE:

King Æthelberht of Kent (560–616): Played a crucial role in the early conversion to Christianity, welcoming Augustine of Canterbury to Kent.

Alfred the Great (849–899): King of Wessex, defended England against Viking invasions, known for military successes, legal reforms, and commitment to learning.

Æthelstan (895–939): The first King of England, consolidated the Anglo-Saxon kingdoms into a unified realm.

Dunstan (909–988): Archbishop of Canterbury, influential in the monastic reform movement, advisor to several Anglo-Saxon kings.

Harold Godwinson (1022–1066): The last Anglo-Saxon king of England, ascended to the throne in 1066, defeated at the Battle of Hastings.

William the Conqueror (1028–1087): Duke of Normandy, victor at the Battle of Hastings in 1066, became the first Norman King of England.

Ragnar Lothbrok: Legendary Norse hero and warrior associated with Viking sagas.

Canute the Great (995–1035): Norse king, ruled England, Denmark, and Norway, marked a period of stability and cultural exchange.

Harald Hardrada (1015–1066): Norwegian king and warrior, sought the English throne, defeated at the Battle of Stamford Bridge.

PLACES:

Wessex: Anglo-Saxon kingdom with its capital at Winchester, played a pivotal role in resisting Viking invasions.

Jarrow and Wearmouth Monasteries: Centres of learning, home to scholars like Bede, providing valuable insights into the history and culture of the time.

Danelaw: Region in England under Viking control, had its own legal code and customs distinct from the rest of Anglo-Saxon England.

Canterbury: Important ecclesiastical centre, seat of the Archbishop of Canterbury, starting point of Augustine's mission.

York (Jorvik): A Viking stronghold, significant city in the Danelaw.

EVENTS:

Augustine's Mission (597): Beginning of the Christianisation of Anglo-Saxon England, led by Augustine of Canterbury.

Viking Raids (8th–11th centuries): Series of raids and invasions by Vikings, contributing to the eventual unification of England.

Alfred's Defence against Vikings (9th century): Successful defence by Alfred the Great, including the Battle of Edington, securing the survival of Anglo-Saxon England.

Battle of Stamford Bridge (1066): Fought between English forces led by Harold Godwinson and Norwegian invaders, preceding the Battle of Hastings.

Battle of Hastings (1066): William the Conqueror's victory marking the end of the Anglo-Saxon era and the beginning of Norman rule in England.

Raid on Lindisfarne (793): First recorded Viking raid in England, symbolising the start of widespread attacks.

Battle of Edington (878): Alfred the Great's decisive victory against the Vikings, leading to the Treaty of Wedmore.

Viking Great Army (865–878): Large Viking force that invaded and occupied parts of England, shaping the Danelaw.

CHAPTER 4 - NORMAN CONQUEST AND MEDIEVAL ENGLAND

1066 - 1485

The Norman Conquest of England in 1066 was a pivotal moment in the nation's history, marking the beginning of a new era under the rule of William the Conqueror. This event brought about significant changes in governance, culture, and society, shaping the course of medieval England until the end of the Plantagenet dynasty in 1485.

Battle of Hastings (Bayeux Tapestry)

William, Duke of Normandy, claimed the English throne after the death of King Edward the Confessor. The Battle of Hastings in 1066 saw the decisive clash between William's forces and the English army led by Harold Godwinson. William emerged victorious, leading to his coronation as King William I of England on Christmas Day 1066.

The Norman Conquest resulted in the imposition of Norman feudalism on England. William redistributed land among his loyal supporters, consolidating his power and creating a new aristocratic class. The Domesday Book, a comprehensive survey of landownership and resources, was commissioned by William to facilitate efficient taxation and governance.

The medieval period under the Plantagenet era, which spanned from 1154 to 1485, witnessed significant political and social developments. The reign of Henry II marked the establishment of a strong central government and the introduction of legal reforms, including the development of common law. The conflict between Henry II and Thomas Becket, the Archbishop of Canterbury, underscored tensions between the monarchy and the Church.

The Plantagenet era was also marked by military conflicts, including the Hundred Years' War with France. Notable figures like Richard the Lionheart and Edward III played key roles in these conflicts, while Joan of Arc emerged as a symbol of resistance for the French.

Economic changes during this period saw the growth of trade and the rise of a merchant class. The Black Death in the 14th century had a profound impact, leading to a significant reduction in the population and triggering social and economic upheavals.

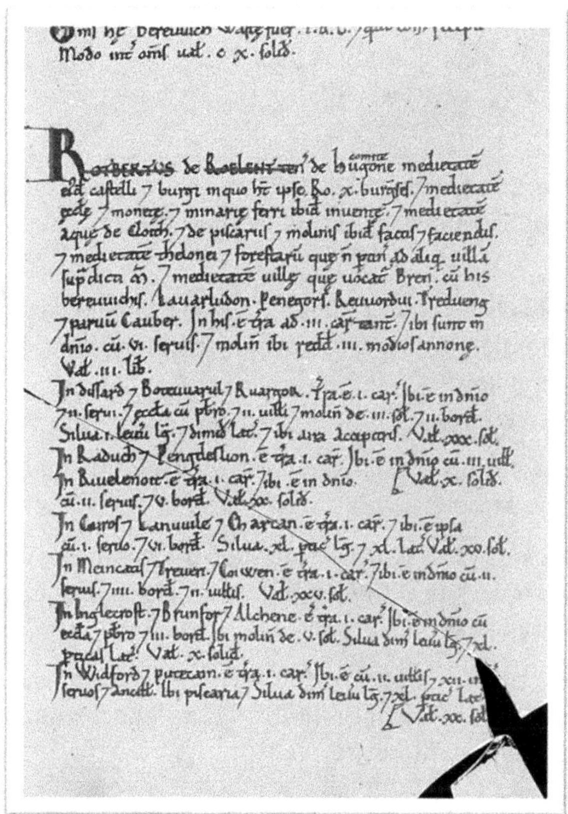

A Page from the Doomsday Book Manuscripts

The Norman Conquest and the medieval period under the Plantagenet dynasty shaped the foundations of England, leaving a lasting impact on its political, social, and economic landscape. The era was marked by power struggles, legal developments, military conflicts, and significant demographic changes, laying the groundwork for the subsequent chapters in English history.

IMPORTANT PEOPLE, PLACES AND EVENTS DURING THIS PERIOD

PEOPLE:

William the Conqueror (1028-1087): Duke of Normandy and the conqueror of England in 1066. He became the first Norman king of England.

Harold Godwinson (1022-1066): The last Anglo-Saxon king of England who died at the Battle of Hastings, leading to William the Conqueror's victory.

Henry II (1133-1189): The first Plantagenet king, known for strengthening the central government, legal reforms, and the conflict with Thomas Becket.

Thomas Becket (1118-1170): Archbishop of Canterbury who clashed with Henry II over the authority of the Church, leading to his murder in Canterbury Cathedral.

Richard the Lionheart (1157-1199): Son of Henry II, known for his military exploits during the Third Crusade and his absence from England for much of his reign.

Edward III (1312-1377): A key figure during the Hundred Years' War, known for his military successes and the establishment of the Order of the Garter.

Joan of Arc (1412-1431): A French heroine who played a crucial role in the Hundred Years' War, leading the French army to several victories before being captured and executed.

PLACES:

Battle of Hastings (1066): Fought between the Normans and English, this battle marked the beginning of Norman rule in England.

Canterbury Cathedral: Site of the murder of Thomas Becket in 1170 and a significant religious and pilgrimage centre.

The Tower of London: Originally built by William the Conqueror, it became a symbol of royal power and a place of imprisonment and execution.

Borough Market (established in the 12th century): One of London's oldest markets, reflecting the growing importance of trade during the medieval period.

Agincourt (1415): A significant English victory during the Hundred Years' War, led by Henry V, against the French.

Bosworth Field (1485): The site of the Battle of Bosworth, where Henry VII defeated Richard III, marking the end of the Wars of the Roses.

EVENTS:

The Domesday Book (1086): Commissioned by William the Conqueror, it was a comprehensive survey of landownership and resources in England.

Magna Carta (1215): Signed by King John, it limited the powers of the monarchy and laid the foundation for constitutional principles.

Hundred Years' War (1337-1453): A series of conflicts between England and France, with notable battles like Crecy, Poitiers, and Agincourt.

The Black Death (1348-1350): A devastating pandemic that significantly reduced the population and had profound social and economic consequences.

CHAPTER 5 - THE WARS OF THE ROSES

1455-1487 A.D.

A series of civil wars fought between the rival houses of Lancaster and York for control of the English throne.

The Wars of the Roses, spanning from 1455 to 1487 A.D., were a tumultuous and complex series of conflicts that engulfed England, marking a pivotal period in its history. This dynastic struggle between the rival houses of Lancaster and York sought to determine the rightful claim to the English throne.

The roots of the conflict can be traced back to the strained relations between the descendants of Edward III. The Lancastrian claim, represented by the red rose, and the Yorkist claim, symbolised by the white rose, became emblematic of the deep-seated divisions within the aristocracy.

The spark that ignited the Wars of the Roses was the dispute over the legitimacy of King Henry VI's rule. The Lancastrian monarch faced challenges from the House of York, led by figures such as Richard, Duke of York, who contested the validity of Henry's reign.

The battles of St Albans (1455), Towton (1461), Barnet (1471), Tewkesbury (1471) and Bosworth (1485) were significant clashes that defined the course of the conflict. Towton, in particular, stands out as one of the bloodiest battles in English history, resulting in a decisive Yorkist victory under Edward IV.

Battle of Tewkesbury 1471

The Wars of the Roses also witnessed the emergence of key personalities, including Richard III, whose reign was marked by controversy and ultimately culminated in his defeat at the Battle of Bosworth. It was on this battlefield in 1485 that Henry Tudor, the Lancastrian claimant, emerged victorious, leading to the establishment of the Tudor dynasty.

The impact of the Wars of the Roses was far-reaching, shaping the political landscape and laying the groundwork for the subsequent Tudor era. The conflict left an indelible mark on the nation, with its repercussions echoing through the centuries of British history.

IMPORTANT PEOPLE, PLACES AND EVENTS DURING THIS PERIOD

PEOPLE:

Henry VI (1421–1471): A Lancastrian king whose reign was marked by political instability, paving the way for the Wars of the Roses. His bouts of mental illness and weak leadership contributed to the tensions.

Edward IV (1442–1483): A prominent Yorkist leader who secured the throne after the Battle of Towton in 1461. Edward's reign was characterised by relative stability, though internal conflicts within the Yorkist camp persisted.

Richard, Duke of York (1411–1460): An influential Yorkist claimant to the throne and father of Edward IV. His death at the Battle of Wakefield in 1460 intensified the hostilities.

Margaret of Anjou (1430–1482): Queen consort of Henry VI and a key figure in the Lancastrian cause. She played an active role in the politics of the era, fiercely defending her husband's claim.

Richard III (1452–1485): The last Yorkist king, known for his controversial reign and ultimate defeat at the Battle of Bosworth. His death marked the end of the Wars of the Roses and the rise of the Tudor dynasty.

Henry Tudor (1457–1509): Earl of Richmond and later Henry VII, he emerged victorious at the Battle of Bosworth, uniting the Lancastrian and Yorkist claims and establishing the Tudor dynasty.

PLACES:

St Albans: The site of the first battle in 1455, marking the initial armed conflict between the houses of Lancaster and York.

Towton: Fought in 1461, this battle was the largest and bloodiest of the Wars of the Roses, resulting in a decisive Yorkist victory and the coronation of Edward IV.

Barnet: The Battle of Barnet in 1471 saw a Yorkist victory under Edward IV, leading to the death of Richard Neville, Earl of Warwick, a key Lancastrian supporter.

Bosworth: The Battle of Bosworth in 1485 was the final clash of the Wars of the Roses. Henry Tudor defeated Richard III, ascending to the throne as Henry VII.

EVENTS:

First Battle of St Albans (1455): The opening battle of the Wars of the Roses, where the conflict between the Lancastrians and Yorkists erupted.

Battle of Towton (1461): A pivotal engagement resulting in a decisive Yorkist victory and the establishment of Edward IV as king.

Warwick's Rebellion (1470-1471): The Earl of Warwick's shifting allegiances and rebellion against Edward IV, culminating in his death at the Battle of Barnet.

Richard III's Reign (1483-1485): Richard III's controversial rule, marked by the disappearance of the Princes in the Tower and the Battle of Bosworth.

Battle of Bosworth (1485): The final battle of the Wars of the Roses, leading to Henry Tudor's victory and the beginning of the Tudor dynasty.

CHAPTER 6 - TUDOR ENGLAND

1485-1603 A.D.

Tudor England emerges as a compelling chapter spanning from 1485 to 1603, marked by the reigns of monarchs who navigated the intricate maze of political, religious, and societal transformations.

Portrait of King Henry VII

Henry VII's ascension in 1485, after his triumph at the Battle of Bosworth, inaugurated a period of stabilisation. Through prudent financial policies and the establishment of the Court of Star Chamber, Henry VII consolidated power, uniting the warring houses of Lancaster and York.

The Family of King Henry VIII

The subsequent reign of Henry VIII ushered in a transformative era. His fervent desire for a male heir led to the Act of Supremacy in 1534, marking the establishment of the Church of England and the English Reformation. The dissolution of monasteries and the creation of the Royal Navy showcased Henry's profound impact on religious and military affairs.

Upon Henry VIII's death, his young son Edward VI briefly ascended the throne, pushing further Protestant reforms. The subsequent rule of Mary I, a devout Catholic, saw a return to Catholicism and earned her the epithet "Bloody Mary" due to her persecution of Protestants.

William Shakespeare

The height of the Tudor dynasty unfolded under Elizabeth I Her court became a flourishing centre for literature, with luminaries like William Shakespeare contributing to the Elizabethan Renaissance. The Elizabethan Religious Settlement in 1559 sought to strike a religious balance, and the defeat of the Spanish Armada in 1588 solidified England's naval supremacy.

Beneath the surface of political grandeur, Tudor England grappled with profound social and economic changes. A burgeoning population led to urbanisation challenges, while the enclosure movement displaced rural communities, sparking social tensions.

As the century unfolded, England ventured into exploration and expansion. Figures like Sir Walter Raleigh and Sir Francis Drake expanded England's global reach, laying the groundwork for future colonial endeavours.

Sir Walter Raleigh

In essence, Tudor England stands as an era of dynamic shifts, where political intrigue, religious upheaval, and societal changes wove together to create an intricate picture that has left an indelible mark on the history of the British Isles. This chapter, with its intricate blend of events, continues to shape the legacy of the Tudor era in the annals of history.

IMPORTANT PEOPLE, PLACES AND EVENTS DURING THIS PERIOD

PEOPLE:

Henry VII (r. 1485–1509): Founder of the Tudor dynasty, he brought stability after the Wars of the Roses. Established the Court of Star Chamber and focused on financial stability.

Henry VIII (r. 1509–1547): Oversaw the English Reformation and established the Church of England. Conducted six marriages, leading to political and religious consequences. Strengthened the Royal Navy and engaged in military campaigns.

Elizabeth I (r. 1558–1603): Oversaw the Elizabethan Religious Settlement, balancing Catholic and Protestant elements. Presided over a flourishing cultural period, known as the Elizabethan Renaissance. Successfully defended England against the Spanish Armada in 1588.

Edward VI (r. 1547–1553): Son of Henry VIII, initiated further Protestant reforms during his short reign.

Mary I (r. 1553–1558): Attempted to restore Catholicism, earning the epithet "Bloody Mary" for her persecution of Protestants.

William Shakespeare: The renowned playwright and poet of the Elizabethan era, contributing significantly to English literature.

Sir Walter Raleigh: Explorer and courtier who sponsored the Roanoke Colony and contributed to the expansion of England's influence.

Sir Francis Drake: Renowned naval captain and explorer; completed the second circumnavigation of the globe.

PLACES:

Court of Star Chamber: Established by Henry VII, it became a royal court dealing with matters of justice and law.

The Royal Navy: Expanded under Henry VIII, becoming a formidable naval force.

The Mary Rose: Flagship of Henry VIII's navy, sunk in 1545 during the Battle of the Solent.

The Roanoke Colony: Sponsored by Sir Walter Raleigh, one of the first attempts at English colonisation in the Americas.

The Spanish Armada: Defeated by the English navy in 1588, a pivotal moment in Tudor history that enhanced England's maritime reputation.

EVENTS:

Battle of Bosworth (1485): Henry VII's victory, marking the end of the Wars of the Roses and the beginning of Tudor rule.

Act of Supremacy (1534): Declared Henry VIII as the Supreme Head of the Church of England, initiating the English Reformation.

Dissolution of the Monasteries (1536–1541): Henry VIII's policy to dissolve monasteries, redistributing wealth and altering the religious landscape.

Elizabethan Religious Settlement (1559): Attempted to strike a religious balance, defining the Church of England's structure during Elizabeth I's reign.

Defeat of the Spanish Armada (1588): A naval victory for England, securing its dominance in maritime affairs.

Exploration and Circumnavigation (late 16th century): Expeditions by explorers like Sir Walter Raleigh and Sir Francis Drake expanded England's global reach.

CHAPTER 7 - STUART ENGLAND

1603-1714 A.D.

The Stuart era in England, spanning from 1603 to 1714 A.D., encapsulates a rich mosaic of political, cultural, and religious developments that left an indelible mark on British history. This period unfolded in a series of interconnected events, shaping the destiny of the nation.

The reign of James I, beginning in 1603, marked the unification of the English and Scottish crowns, ushering in the Jacobean era. This period witnessed a cultural renaissance with the literary brilliance of William Shakespeare and the production of the King James Version of the Bible. The court of James I became a centre for artistic expression and intellectual pursuits.

As the mantle passed to Charles I in 1625, tensions between the monarchy and Parliament escalated. The struggle for power culminated in the outbreak of the English Civil War in 1642. The conflict, characterised by pivotal battles like Marston Moor and Naseby, ultimately led to the execution of Charles I in 1649, heralding the onset of the Interregnum.

The Interregnum, under the rule of Oliver Cromwell, witnessed a radical shift in governance. England became a republic, and strict moral codes were enforced. The closure of theatres marked a departure from the cultural vibrancy of the previous era. Despite these challenges, the Interregnum also saw the development of new political ideas and the flourishing of Puritan literature.

The Execution of King Charles I

The political landscape underwent a significant transformation with the Restoration in 1660. Charles II ascended to the throne, bringing about a resurgence of cultural and artistic expression. Theatres reopened, and the arts flourished with the emergence of Restoration comedy. However, political tensions persisted, compounded by Charles II's Catholic sympathies and the implementation of the Test Acts.

James II's attempt to promote Catholicism and consolidate royal power sparked the Glorious Revolution of 1688. William III and Mary II ascended to the throne with parliamentary support, leading to constitutional changes. The Bill of Rights in 1689 defined the relationship between the monarchy and Parliament, laying the foundation for a constitutional monarchy.

The Bill of Rights Ratified at the Revolution by King William, and Queen Mary

The early 18th century, under Queen Anne's reign, witnessed the consolidation of parliamentary power. The Act of Union with Scotland in 1707 created the Kingdom of Great Britain, unifying the two nations politically. Queen Anne's era also saw the expansion of the British Empire, particularly in the context of the War of Spanish Succession.

Queen Anne

The Stuart period in England is a saga of political upheavals, cultural brilliance, and constitutional transformations. Its influence reverberates through British history, shaping the nation's identity and governance for centuries to come.

IMPORTANT PEOPLE, PLACES AND EVENTS DURING THIS PERIOD

PEOPLE:

James I (1567–1625): The first monarch of the Stuart dynasty, James I's reign saw the unification of the English and Scottish crowns in 1603. A patron of the arts, he played a significant role in the Jacobean era.

Charles I (1600–1649): The son of James I, Charles I's reign was marked by escalating tensions with Parliament, leading to the English Civil War. His execution in 1649 marked a turning point in English history.

Oliver Cromwell (1599–1658): A military and political leader, Cromwell played a central role in the Interregnum. As Lord Protector, he ruled over the Commonwealth of England, Scotland, and Ireland.

Charles II (1630–1685): The "Merry Monarch," Charles II's reign marked the Restoration era. His return to the throne in 1660 brought about a resurgence of the arts and the reopening of theatres.

James II (1633–1701): James II's Catholic sympathies and attempts to consolidate royal power led to the Glorious Revolution. His deposition paved the way for constitutional changes in 1688.

William III (1650–1702) and Mary II (1662–1694): Ascending to the throne after the Glorious Revolution, this joint monarch pair played a crucial role in establishing constitutional monarchy and signed the Bill of Rights in 1689.

Queen Anne (1665–1714): The last Stuart monarch, Anne's reign witnessed the Act of Union with Scotland in 1707, creating the Kingdom of Great Britain.

PLACES:

Whitehall Palace: The primary residence of the English monarchs, including James I and Charles I. It was a centre of political and cultural activities during the Stuart era.

Edgehill: The site of the first major battle of the English Civil War in 1642, fought between Royalist and Parliamentarian forces.

Naseby: The location of a decisive battle in 1645 during the English Civil War, resulting in a Parliamentarian victory and shaping the course of the conflict.

London: The capital city, which witnessed political upheavals, the restoration of the monarchy, and cultural renaissance during this period.

Westminster Abbey: A significant location for coronations and burials, Westminster Abbey played a role in various events, including the Glorious Revolution.

EVENTS:

Union of the Crowns (1603): James I's ascension to the throne united the English and Scottish crowns, creating the Kingdom of Great Britain in 1707.

English Civil War (1642–1651): A series of conflicts between Royalists and Parliamentarians, resulting in the execution of Charles I and the establishment of the Commonwealth.

Interregnum (1649–1660): The period of republican rule under Oliver Cromwell, marked by political and religious changes.

Restoration (1660): The return of the monarchy under Charles II, bringing about a cultural and artistic revival.

Glorious Revolution (1688): William III and Mary II's ascent to the throne, leading to constitutional changes and the establishment of a constitutional monarchy.

Act of Union (1707): The union between England and Scotland, forming the Kingdom of Great Britain under Queen Anne.

CHAPTER 8 - GEORGIAN ERA

1714–1837 A.D.

The Georgian Era, spanning from 1714 to 1837 A.D., was a profound and multifaceted chapter in the history of Britain, marked by significant political, social, cultural, and economic transformations. This period, named after the four consecutive Hanoverian monarchs named George, unfolded as a rich mixture of events that shaped the nation's trajectory.

The era commenced with the Hanoverian succession in 1714, as George I ascended to the British throne. This marked a pivotal moment, as the Hanoverian monarchs grappled with the challenges of governing in the context of a developing constitutional monarchy. The political landscape witnessed upheavals, and the era saw the evolution of the role of the Prime Minister, with figures like Sir Robert Walpole and William Pitt the Younger playing crucial roles in shaping the government.

Intellectually, the Georgian era coincided with the Age of Enlightenment. Thinkers such as John Locke and David Hume laid the groundwork for political philosophy, contributing to the intellectual ferment of the time. In the literary realm, the era saw the emergence of Samuel Johnson and the publication of the first modern dictionary, symbolising the era's commitment to intellectual advancement.

One of the most transformative aspects of the Georgian era was the Industrial Revolution, which unfolded from the late 18th to the early 19th century. The shift from agrarian to industrial society brought about technological innovations such as the steam engine and mechanised textile production, revolutionising industries and fundamentally altering the economic landscape.

Mechanised Looms During the Industrial Revolution

Colonial expansion was another hallmark of the Georgian era. The Seven Years' War (1756–1763) resulted in territorial gains, including Canada and parts of India. Simultaneously, the establishment and governance of the Thirteen Colonies in North America played a significant role in shaping the global influence of the British Empire.

Culturally, the Georgian era was a time of flourishing creativity. Literary luminaries like Jane Austen and William Blake, along with artists such as Thomas Gainsborough and Joshua Reynolds, contributed to the vibrant cultural scene of the time.

Socially, the era witnessed structural changes in society. The emergence of the middle class, urbanisation, and shifts in family dynamics were notable social transformations. The abolitionist movement gained momentum, signalling changing attitudes towards slavery.

The Regency era, from 1811 to 1820, named after the Prince Regent (later George IV), continued the cultural vibrancy and political stability of the Georgian era. This period is often associated with the elegant Regency style in architecture and fashion.

British Napoleonic Infantry

However, the Georgian era was also marked by challenges, notably the Napoleonic Wars (1803–1815), a series of conflicts that had profound impacts on England's economy, society, and global standing.

The Georgian era concluded with the accession of Queen Victoria in 1837. While her reign officially marked the beginning of the Victorian era, the legacy of the Georgian period continued to influence the cultural, political, and social fabric of Britain.

The Georgian era was a dynamic and transformative period that laid the foundation for many aspects of modern Britain. From political developments and industrialisation to cultural achievements, the legacy of the Georgian era remains deeply embedded in the historical foundations of the nation.

IMPORTANT PEOPLE, PLACES AND EVENTS DURING THIS PERIOD

PEOPLE:

George I (1660–1727): The first Hanoverian monarch of Britain, his accession in 1714 marked the beginning of the Georgian era.

Sir Robert Walpole (1676–1745): Often considered the first de facto Prime Minister, Walpole played a crucial role in stabilising the government and consolidating power.

William Pitt the Younger (1759–1806): A prominent political figure, Pitt served as Prime Minister during crucial times, including the Napoleonic Wars.

John Locke (1632–1704): A philosopher whose ideas on government and individual rights had a profound influence during the Age of Enlightenment.

David Hume (1711–1776): A Scottish philosopher and historian, his works contributed significantly to Enlightenment thought.

Samuel Johnson (1709–1784): A literary figure and compiler of the first comprehensive English dictionary, symbolising intellectual achievements during the era.

Jane Austen (1775–1817): An influential novelist, her works, such as "Pride and Prejudice" and "Sense and Sensibility," captured the social nuances of the time.

Thomas Gainsborough (1727–1788) and Joshua Reynolds (1723–1792): Prominent painters whose works contributed to the cultural vibrancy of the Georgian era.

George IV (1762–1830): The Prince Regent and later King, his reign in the early 19th century is associated with the Regency style.

William IV (1765–1837): The "Sailor King," his reign saw the passage of the Reform Act of 1832, a significant political reform.

Queen Victoria (1819–1901): While her reign officially marked the beginning of the Victorian era, her accession in 1837 concluded the Georgian era.

PLACES:

Westminster: The political centre of Britain, including the Palace of Westminster, where political decisions and debates took place.

Industrial Centres (e.g., Manchester, Birmingham): Hubs of industrialisation during the Industrial Revolution, playing a pivotal role in economic transformations.

Colonial Territories (e.g., India, Canada): Regions that became part of the expanding British Empire, contributing to economic and geopolitical influence.

Literary and Cultural Hubs (e.g., London coffeehouses, literary salons): Places where intellectuals, writers, and artists gathered to exchange ideas and foster cultural developments.

Regency-era Architectural Sites (e.g., Royal Pavilion in Brighton): Reflective of the elegant Regency style prevalent during the early 19th century.

EVENTS:

Hanoverian Succession (1714): George I ascended to the throne, marking the beginning of the Georgian era.

Industrial Revolution (late 18th to early 19th century): A transformative period marked by advancements in manufacturing, technology, and transportation.

Seven Years' War (1756–1763): A global conflict resulting in significant territorial gains for Britain, including parts of India and Canada.

American War of Independence (1775–1783): The Thirteen Colonies sought independence from British rule, leading to the formation of the United States.

French Revolution (1789–1799): A series of events in France that had significant repercussions across Europe, impacting Britain's political and social landscape.

Napoleonic Wars (1803–1815): A series of conflicts with Napoleon's French Empire that had profound effects on Britain's economy and global standing.

Regency Era (1811–1820): The period when George IV served as Prince Regent, characterised by cultural vibrancy and architectural elegance.

Reform Act of 1832: William IV's reign saw the passage of this significant political reform, extending voting rights and restructuring parliamentary representation.

Queen Victoria's Accession (1837): Marks the official transition from the Georgian to the Victorian era, concluding this transformative period in British history.

CHAPTER 9 - VICTORIAN ENGLAND

1837-1901 A.D.

The Victorian Era, spanning from 1837 to 1901 A.D., stands as a transformative chapter in the history of Britain, marked by profound changes across society, economy, culture, and politics.

In the intricate maze of Victorian society, a rigid class system defined the aristocracy, middle class, and working class, each adhering to distinct social norms. Guiding these societal structures were Victorian values, underpinned by a stringent moral code emphasising virtues such as industriousness, frugality, and family stability.

The ongoing Industrial Revolution continued to reshape the economic landscape, with technological marvels like the steam engine propelling unprecedented industrialisation. Factories proliferated, and cities expanded, fostering increased production and economic prosperity. However, this rapid industrialisation also brought forth challenges, including dismal working conditions, labour exploitation, and crowded urban living.

Scientific and technological progress flourished during the Victorian era, as Charles Darwin's seminal work revolutionised biological thought. Scientific institutions thrived, contributing to advancements in medicine, physics, and chemistry. Simultaneously, intrepid explorers ventured into uncharted territories, expanding the frontiers of human knowledge.

Victorian England reached the peak of its imperial power, extending influence across colonies in Africa, Asia, and the

Pacific. Imperial expansion significantly contributed to Britain's economic affluence, although debates surrounding morality, the ethical responsibilities of an imperial power, and the consequences of colonial exploitation ensued.

Addressing the societal impacts of industrialisation, Victorian reformers championed child labour laws and improved working conditions. Florence Nightingale pioneered transformative healthcare practices, while philanthropic initiatives aimed to alleviate the suffering of the urban poor, reflecting a growing societal awareness of social inequalities.

The Victorian era witnessed a cultural renaissance, with prolific output from writers and artists. Renowned novelists like Charles Dickens and the Brontë sisters addressed social issues, while the Pre-Raphaelite Brotherhood sought to revive medieval aesthetics. Photography emerged as a new medium, capturing the realities of Victorian life.

Architecturally, the era showcased a diverse range of styles, including the Gothic Revival, Italianate, and Queen Anne. The Crystal Palace, constructed for the Great Exhibition of 1851, symbolised the grandeur and innovation of Victorian design.

The Crimean War (1853–1856) marked a significant military conflict during the era, with Britain confronting Russia. This war, characterised by new technologies and military strategies, marked a turning point in military medicine, with Florence Nightingale's pioneering efforts.

The Great Exhibition of 1851, held at the Crystal Palace in London, was a landmark event showcasing Britain's industrial prowess and innovations. It became a symbol of Victorian confidence, celebrating progress and ingenuity.

The Opening of The Great Exhibition, 1st May 1851

Queen Victoria's reign defined the era, influencing cultural and technological advancements. Her marriage to Prince Albert, the Prince Consort, left a lasting impact, while the sombre and conservative aspects of Victorian culture were evident during the extended mourning period following Albert's death in 1861.

Queen Victoria and Prince Albert

In essence, the Victorian era was a complex fate of progress and challenges, shaping the foundations of modern Britain. The legacy of this period continues to resonate, influencing contemporary perceptions of the Victorian age and leaving an enduring impact on societal, economic, and cultural norms.

IMPORTANT PEOPLE, PLACES AND EVENTS DURING THIS PERIOD

PEOPLE:

Queen Victoria (1819–1901): The monarch whose reign defined the era, Queen Victoria played a crucial role in shaping Victorian England. Her marriage to Prince Albert influenced cultural and technological advancements.

Prince Albert (1819–1861): The Prince Consort, husband of Queen Victoria, was a significant figure influencing cultural and technological advancements during the Victorian era.

Charles Dickens (1812–1870): A prolific novelist, Dickens addressed social issues through works like "Oliver Twist" and "Great Expectations," offering insights into Victorian society.

Charlotte Brontë (1816–1855) and Emily Brontë (1818–1848): Renowned novelists, Charlotte's "Jane Eyre" and Emily's "Wuthering Heights" reflected the societal nuances of the time.

Florence Nightingale (1820–1910): A pioneer in nursing, Nightingale revolutionised healthcare practices during the Crimean War and contributed to public health reforms.

Charles Darwin (1809–1882): A naturalist whose theory of evolution, presented in "On the Origin of Species" (1859), had profound implications for biological thought.

Lord Shaftesbury (1801–1885): A social reformer, Shaftesbury advocated for child labour laws and better working conditions during the Victorian era.

Dante Gabriel Rossetti (1828–1882) and John Everett Millais (1829–1896): Founders of the Pre-Raphaelite Brotherhood, contributing to the revival of medieval aesthetics in art.

Isambard Kingdom Brunel (1806–1859): An influential engineer, Brunel played a key role in the construction of railways, bridges, and ships during the Victorian era.

William Gladstone (1809–1898) and Benjamin Disraeli (1804–1881): Prominent political figures, both served as Prime Ministers during Queen Victoria's reign, contributing to political developments.

PLACES:

Crystal Palace (London): Constructed for the Great Exhibition of 1851, the Crystal Palace symbolised the grandeur and innovation of Victorian design.

Colonial Territories (Various): The British Empire expanded its influence across colonies in Africa, Asia, and the Pacific during the era, contributing to economic affluence.

Industrial Centres (Various): Hubs of industrialisation, including cities like Manchester and Birmingham, played a pivotal role in economic transformations.

Crimean Peninsula: The Crimean War (1853–1856) unfolded in this region, with British forces, along with allies, facing off against Russia.

Westminster (London): The political centre of Britain, including the Palace of Westminster, where key political decisions and debates occurred.

EVENTS:

The Great Exhibition of 1851: Held at the Crystal Palace in London, this event showcased Britain's industrial prowess and innovations, becoming a symbol of Victorian confidence.

Crimean War (1853–1856): A significant military conflict involving Britain, France, and the Ottoman Empire against Russia, marked by new technologies and military strategies.

Industrial Revolution (Late 18th to 19th century): A transformative period characterised by technological advancements, factories, and urbanisation.

Reform Acts (1832, 1867, 1884): Legislative reforms extending voting rights and restructuring parliamentary representation, contributing to political changes.

Publication of "On the Origin of Species" (1859): Charles Darwin's groundbreaking work revolutionising biological thought and contributing to the scientific progress of the era.

The Marriage of Queen Victoria and Prince Albert (1840): A significant event influencing cultural and technological advancements during the Victorian era.

Social Reforms and Philanthropy: Ongoing efforts to address societal issues, including child labour laws, improved working conditions, and healthcare reforms championed by figures like Lord Shaftesbury and Florence Nightingale.

CHAPTER 10 - EDWARDIAN ERA

1901-1910 A.D.

The Edwardian Era, spanning from 1901 to 1910 A.D., unfolded in the aftermath of Queen Victoria's demise, marking the ascension of her son, King Edward VII, to the British throne. This era encapsulates a unique blend of continuity from the Victorian times and the emergence of significant societal changes that would go on to define the 20th century.

King Edward VII, often referred to as the "Peacemaker," ushered in a new era characterised by a more relaxed and sociable atmosphere compared to the solemnity of his mother's reign. His influence extended beyond mere governance, shaping the social fabric with his penchant for social events and a cosmopolitan lifestyle.

While the Edwardian Era maintained distinct social hierarchies, there was a perceptible loosening of the rigid class divisions entrenched in the Victorian period. The upper class continued to indulge in luxurious lifestyles, but the expanding middle class exhibited characteristics associated with the upper echelons. Concurrently, efforts to improve working conditions began to manifest within certain sectors of the working class.

Artistic and cultural flourishing defined the Edwardian era. The influence of the Arts and Crafts Movement, rooted in the late Victorian period, persisted, shaping design and aesthetics. Simultaneously, the era witnessed the rise of modernist ideas in literature and the arts, foreshadowing the transformative changes that lay ahead in the 20th century.

King Edward VII in His Coronation Robes

Edwardian fashion epitomised elegance and sophistication. Women's attire featured high collars, corsets, and wide-brimmed hats, while men's fashion embraced tailored suits and formalwear. The opulence of the upper class was reflected in the use of luxurious fabrics and intricate embellishments.

The Edwardian era marked a period of significant technological advancements. Innovations in transportation, including the expansion of railways and the advent of the automobile, reshaped daily life. Moreover, the era witnessed the nascent stages of aviation experimentation, providing a glimpse into the future transformations of the 20th century.

The Titanic Sailing out of Southampton

Although occurring just after the Edwardian era, the sinking of the RMS Titanic had a profound impact on the collective consciousness of the time. The luxury and tragedy of the Titanic epitomised the contradictions and complexities inherent in Edwardian society.

The Arrest of Suffragette Emmeline Pankhurst

Throughout the Edwardian era, Britain maintained its imperial dominance. The pursuit of empire-building and global influence remained central to British foreign policy, leading to territorial expansions in Africa and Asia.

The Edwardian era served as a pivotal period for the women's suffrage movement. Figures like Emmeline Pankhurst led suffragettes in active campaigns for women's right to vote. Tensions escalated, culminating in protests and demonstrations that set the stage for broader suffrage battles in the subsequent decades.

Despite outward prosperity, social challenges persisted. Economic disparities, particularly between classes, fuelled social unrest. Labour strikes and demands for workers' rights underscored the underlying tensions in Edwardian society.

The Edwardian Era, while marked by opulence and cultural vibrancy, also signified the decline of an older world order. The geopolitical landscape was shifting, and the outbreak of World War I in 1914 would signal the end of this era, ushering in a new, tumultuous chapter in history.

In essence, the Edwardian Era was a transitional period that bridged the 19th and 20th centuries. It was characterised by elegance, cultural dynamism, and technological advancements, but it also grappled with the challenges and inequalities that would ultimately contribute to the profound societal changes of the 20th century.

IMPORTANT PEOPLE, PLACES AND EVENTS DURING THIS PERIOD

PEOPLE:

King Edward VII (1841–1910): Ascended to the throne in 1901, his reign marked the Edwardian Era, characterised by a more relaxed and sociable atmosphere.

Emmeline Pankhurst (1858–1928): A leading suffragette, Pankhurst played a pivotal role in the women's suffrage movement, advocating for women's right to vote.

Isambard Kingdom Brunel (1806–1859): An influential engineer from the Victorian era, his legacy persisted into the Edwardian period, symbolising advancements in engineering.

Joseph Chamberlain (1836–1914): A prominent politician, Chamberlain's influence extended into the Edwardian era, particularly regarding imperial issues and social reform.

George V (1865–1936): Succeeded Edward VII in 1910, his reign extended into the First World War, marking the later part of the Edwardian era.

PLACES:

Crystal Palace (London): Symbolising the grandeur of the Victorian era, remnants of its influence lingered into the Edwardian period, representing a bygone era of innovation.

Westminster (London): The political heart of Britain, where key decisions and debates unfolded, maintaining its significance into the Edwardian period.

Colonial Territories (Various): Imperial influence persisted, with ongoing developments and challenges in British colonies in Africa, Asia, and the Pacific.

Suffrage Headquarters (London): The focal point for suffragette activities, including Emmeline Pankhurst's leadership in the fight for women's voting rights.

Industrial Centres (Various): Hubs of technological and economic progress, witnessing continued advancements during the Edwardian era.

EVENTS:

Death of Queen Victoria (1901): Signalled the end of the Victorian era, leading to the ascension of King Edward VII and the beginning of the Edwardian era.

Women's Suffrage Movement (Early 20th Century): Intensified during the Edwardian era, marked by protests, demonstrations, and increased visibility of suffragette activities.

RMS Titanic Sinking (1912): Although occurring just after the Edwardian era, the tragedy had a profound impact, symbolising the contradictions of opulence and vulnerability.

Technological Advancements (Early 20th Century): Ongoing progress in transportation, including the expansion of railways and experimentation with early aviation technologies.

Imperialism and Territorial Expansion (Early 20th Century): Continued imperial pursuits with developments and challenges in colonies, reflecting Britain's global influence.

Political Reforms (Early 20th Century): Social and political changes, including debates on labour rights and reforms initiated by politicians like Joseph Chamberlain.

Death of King Edward VII (1910): Signified the end of the Edwardian era, with his son George V taking the throne and overseeing the nation into the First World War.

CHAPTER 11 - WORLD WAR I AND INTERWAR PERIOD

1914-1939 A.D.

The 20th century opened with an era of unprecedented global upheaval, marked by the cataclysmic events of World War I and the tumultuous Interwar Period. This chapter unravels the intricacies of this turbulent time, delving into the multifaceted dimensions of conflict, societal transformations, and the seeds of subsequent global challenges.

The origins of World War I lay in a complex palate of political alliances, nationalistic fervor, and simmering tensions among European powers. The assassination of Archduke Franz Ferdinand of Austria-Hungary in 1914 acted as the spark that ignited the powder keg, leading to the declaration of war across the continent.

The war unfolded with the grim reality of trench warfare, where soldiers endured harsh conditions within intricate networks of trenches. Technological advancements, including machine guns, tanks, and chemical warfare, transformed the nature of combat, resulting in staggering casualties and forever altering the face of warfare.

The war's reverberations extended far beyond the battlefields, seeping into the home front where civilians faced rationing, propaganda, and social upheaval. Women, in unprecedented numbers, entered the workforce, contributing to the war effort and laying the groundwork for shifts in societal norms.

World War I Trench Warfare in Somme 1916

As the conflict concluded, the Treaty of Versailles was drafted, imposing harsh conditions on Germany. The punitive nature of the treaty sowed the seeds for future geopolitical tensions and economic hardships, contributing to the rise of extremist ideologies that would define the interwar years.

The post-war era began with economic turmoil, but amidst the hardships emerged the vibrant cultural era of the "Roaring Twenties." Jazz music, flapper fashion, and technological advancements defined this period of relative prosperity, particularly in the United States.

The economic exuberance of the 1920s came crashing down with the Wall Street Crash of 1929, ushering in the Great Depression. Widespread unemployment, poverty, and social distress became pervasive, amplifying existing political tensions.

In the aftermath of World War I and the economic fallout, totalitarian regimes gained traction. The ascent of figures like Adolf Hitler in Germany, Benito Mussolini in Italy, and Joseph Stalin in the Soviet Union exemplified the rise of authoritarian rule, each with its own unique ideology and methods of control.

Fascist ideologies, characterised by extreme nationalism and authoritarianism, took root across Europe. Italy and Germany, in particular, embraced militarism, with expansionist ambitions leading to conflicts like the Italian invasion of Ethiopia and the German occupation of the Rhineland.

The Spanish Civil War unfolded as a precursor to World War II, with the Nationalists, led by Francisco Franco, prevailing over the Republicans. This conflict served as a testing ground for new military strategies and technologies that would shape the impending global conflict.

The policy of appeasement, a strategy to avoid conflict by yielding to aggressive actions, proved ineffective in deterring Hitler's expansionist ambitions. The annexation of Austria, the Munich Agreement, and the invasion of Poland in 1939 marked the prelude to World War II, casting a shadow over a world still reeling from the scars of the Great War.

The period from World War I through the Interwar Years was a tumultuous chapter in human history, defined by the unimaginable toll of global conflict, the societal and cultural shifts of the interwar era, and the ominous rise of totalitarian regimes that set the stage for a more catastrophic global conflagration. The echoes of this period continue to reverberate, shaping the geopolitical landscape and collective memory of the 20th century

The German–Soviet Invasion of Poland 1939

.

IMPORTANT PEOPLE, PLACES AND EVENTS DURING THIS PERIOD

PEOPLE:

Woodrow Wilson (1856–1924): The President of the United States during World War I, Wilson played a crucial role in formulating the League of Nations and the Treaty of Versailles.

Archduke Franz Ferdinand (1863–1914): His assassination in 1914 triggered the chain of events leading to the outbreak of World War I.

Emmeline Pankhurst (1858–1928): A leading suffragette in the UK, Pankhurst advocated for women's rights during and after World War I.

Adolf Hitler (1889–1945): The Nazi leader rose to power in Germany during the interwar period, leading to the outbreak of World War II.

Benito Mussolini (1883–1945): The founder of Italian Fascism, Mussolini became the Prime Minister of Italy and played a key role in the rise of totalitarian regimes.

Joseph Stalin (1878–1953): Rising to power in the Soviet Union, Stalin implemented policies that transformed the nation into an industrial power.

Franklin D. Roosevelt (1882–1945): The President of the United States during the Great Depression and the early years of World War II.

PLACES:

Versailles (France): The Palace of Versailles hosted the signing of the Treaty of Versailles in 1919, marking the formal end of World War I.

The Western Front: A network of trenches stretching across Western Europe where much of the intense fighting occurred during World War I.

Wall Street (New York): The epicentre of the global economic collapse following the Wall Street Crash of 1929, leading to the Great Depression.

Abyssinia (Ethiopia): Mussolini's Italy invaded Abyssinia in 1935, marking a significant event leading up to World War II.

The Rhineland (Germany): Hitler's occupation of the Rhineland in 1936 violated the Treaty of Versailles and foreshadowed further aggression.

EVENTS:

Assassination of Archduke Franz Ferdinand (1914): The event that triggered the beginning of World War I.

Treaty of Versailles (1919): The peace treaty that officially ended World War I, imposing harsh conditions on Germany.

Roaring Twenties (1920s): A period of cultural and social dynamism, particularly in the United States, characterised by economic prosperity and cultural innovation.

Wall Street Crash (1929): The abrupt collapse of the stock market, triggering the Great Depression.

Spanish Civil War (1936–1939): A conflict in Spain between Republicans and Nationalists, serving as a precursor to World War II.

Anschluss (1938): The annexation of Austria into Nazi Germany, violating the Treaty of Versailles.

Munich Agreement (1938): The appeasement policy allowing Hitler's annexation of the Sudetenland, a region of Czechoslovakia.

Invasion of Poland (1939): The event marking the official start of World War II as Germany invaded Poland.

CHAPTER 12 - WORLD WAR II

1939–1945 A.D.

England during World War II emerges as a riveting chapter, etched with the indomitable spirit of a nation thrust into the crucible of global conflict. The nuanced complexity of this period unfolds as a profound narrative, incorporating courage, strategic acumen, and the unyielding resilience of a people confronted by the relentless march of war.

As the world teetered on the brink of turmoil, England found itself confronting an existential crisis. Neville Chamberlain's diplomatic forerunning attempts had faltered, and on September 3, 1939, Britain's solemn declaration of war on Germany marked the commencement of a struggle that would redefine the nation's destiny.

Above the verdant landscapes and quaint villages, the skies became a theatre of defiance during the Battle of Britain. From July to October 1940, the Royal Air Force, with their iconic Spitfires and Hurricanes, engaged in an aerial ballet against the relentless Luftwaffe. This epic clash not only thwarted Hitler's ambitions but underscored the pivotal role of air power in shaping the modern theatre of war.

The Blitz, a relentless bombing campaign, brought war to the doorsteps of English civilians. Cities like London and Coventry bore the scars of nightly raids, yet amidst the rubble, the Home Front emerged as a crucible of fortitude. Air-raid shelters, rationing, and the evacuation of children to the countryside became integral facets of this resilient time.

Spitfire and Hurricane from The Battle of Britain

The shores of Dunkirk witnessed a miraculous evacuation in 1940. Operation Dynamo, executed with meticulous precision, rescued a multitude of stranded troops. The "Dunkirk Spirit," a collective determination to defy overwhelming odds, became a touchstone for the nation, illustrating that even in apparent defeat, victory could be wrested from the jaws of calamity.

Beyond its shores, England's commitment extended to the deserts of North Africa. Field Marshal Bernard Montgomery's leadership spearheaded campaigns against Axis forces, with the Battle of El Alamein in 1942 marking a pivotal turning point.

June 6, 1944, unfolded as an extraordinary chapter as England played a pivotal role in the Allied invasion of Normandy, codenamed D-Day. The meticulous planning and execution of this monumental offensive reflected England's strategic prowess, marking a decisive step towards the liberation of Western Europe.

London's St Paul's Cathedral after The Blitz

In the aftermath of the war, England grappled with the devastating power of the atomic bomb. The bombings of Hiroshima and Nagasaki in August 1945 hastened Japan's surrender, concluding a conflict that had reshaped the very fabric of the world.

The legacy of World War II lingered in the winds of change. Standing amidst the ruins, England forged a new path. The establishment of the welfare state and the National Health Service (NHS) became monuments to a commitment to social progress, rising from the crucible of conflict with a vision for a more egalitarian society.

This chapter of England through World War II stands as a nuanced narrative, a testament to sacrifice, innovation, and endurance. From the cockpit of a Spitfire to the deserts of North Africa, the English experience in this era resonates with the echoes of a nation tested, tempered, and ultimately triumphant in the face of one of the most challenging eras in human history.

IMPORTANT PEOPLE, PLACES AND EVENTS DURING THIS PERIOD

PEOPLE:

Winston Churchill (1874–1965): Prime Minister of the United Kingdom during most of World War II, Churchill's stirring speeches and leadership became synonymous with England's resilience.

Neville Chamberlain (1869–1940): British Prime Minister at the outbreak of the war, Chamberlain's appeasement policy towards Hitler faced criticism, leading to his resignation.

Field Marshal Bernard Montgomery (1887–1976): A prominent British military commander, Montgomery played a pivotal role in North Africa and commanded Allied forces during the Battle of Normandy.

King George VI (1895–1952) and Queen Elizabeth (1900–2002): The royal couple symbolised the steadfastness of the monarchy during the war, providing moral support to the nation.

RAF Pilots (e.g., Douglas Bader, Guy Gibson): The brave pilots of the Royal Air Force, including notable figures like Douglas Bader and Guy Gibson, played a crucial role in the Battle of Britain.

Alan Turing (1912–1954): A mathematician and codebreaker, Turing's work at Bletchley Park contributed significantly to breaking the German Enigma code.

PLACES:

Dunkirk (France): The site of the miraculous evacuation in 1940, where Allied forces were rescued from the beaches.

Bletchley Park (England): The central site for British codebreakers, where the Enigma code was decrypted, contributing to Allied intelligence.

London: Endured extensive bombing during the Blitz, and the resilience of Londoners became emblematic of the Home Front.

Normandy (France): The location of the D-Day landings on June 6, 1944, a pivotal moment in the Allied invasion of Western Europe.

North Africa (e.g., El Alamein, Tobruk): The theatre of operations where British forces, led by Montgomery, engaged Axis forces in crucial battles.

EVENTS:

Declaration of War (1939): Britain's formal declaration of war on Germany on September 3, 1939, in response to the invasion of Poland.

Battle of Britain (1940): The aerial conflict between the RAF and the Luftwaffe, a turning point in thwarting German plans for invasion.

The Blitz (1940–1941): Sustained bombing raids over British cities, particularly London, by the Luftwaffe.

Evacuation of Dunkirk (1940): Operation Dynamo, the mass evacuation of Allied troops from Dunkirk, showcasing resilience amidst apparent defeat.

D-Day (1944): The Allied invasion of Normandy on June 6, 1944, marked a pivotal moment in the liberation of Western Europe.

Atomic Bombings (1945): The dropping of atomic bombs on Hiroshima and Nagasaki in August 1945, leading to Japan's surrender.

CHAPTER 13 - POST-WAR RECONSTRUCTION

1945-1950S A.D.

In the aftermath of the cataclysmic upheaval of World War II, England found itself standing on the precipice of transformation. The end of conflict signalled not just a ceasefire but the onset of an arduous yet remarkable journey — the post-war reconstruction era. Stretching into the 1950s, this period unfolded as a fabric woven with threads of resilience, renewal, and the forging of a nation reborn.

As the echoes of conflict faded, England surveyed a landscape marked by the scars of relentless bombings. Iconic cities lay in ruin, silent witnesses to the toll exacted by war. Yet, amidst the debris, a nation grappling with the aftermath began to gather its collective strength.

In the corridors of power, under the visionary leadership of Prime Minister Clement Attlee, a radical experiment in social reform took root. The post-war Labour government embarked on a transformative journey that went beyond the reconstruction of physical structures. The establishment of the National Health Service (NHS) in 1948 became the embodiment of a new vision, promising healthcare as an inalienable right for all citizens. Social security measures, such as the National Insurance Act, laid the foundation for a society founded on compassion and equity.

The housing crisis demanded audacious solutions. The Housing Acts of 1946 and 1957 set in motion an ambitious endeavour to provide not just homes but communities. Council estates and the emergence of post-war suburbs reshaped the urban fabric, symbolising not just the reconstruction of bricks and mortar but the revival of shattered lives.

The First Day of the National Health Service in 1948

In the realm of education, a renaissance unfolded. The 1944 Education Act, a visionary decree, paved the way for universal and free schooling for every child. The establishment of the Open University in 1969 broke down the hallowed gates of higher education, allowing knowledge to flow freely across societal strata.

The war had spurred technological leaps, and the post-war years witnessed England orchestrating an industrial revival. The

Festival of Britain in 1951 became a grand exposition of the nation's technological prowess and cultural vibrancy. Industries experienced a renaissance, with the automotive and aviation sectors reaching new heights. Television, the mesmerising storyteller in every household, reshaped cultural experiences, knitting communities together into a shared national narrative.

Festival of Britain Tapestry Souvenir 1951

Amidst the socio-economic reconstruction, a cultural renaissance flourished. The "Swinging Sixties," an era of youth culture, vibrant fashion, and revolutionary music, dawned in the 1950s. The arrival of the Windrush generation from the Caribbean infused England's identity with a richness that transcended geographical borders.

The Windrush Generation in the 1950s

Economically, England sought to rebuild and reposition itself on the global stage. International collaborations, such as the Marshall Plan, provided crucial financial aid for reconstruction efforts. England's commitment extended beyond its borders, engaging in the reconstruction of war-torn Europe.

The post-war reconstruction era was more than a mere physical rebuilding; it was an intricate fabric woven with the threads of resilience, vision, and societal metamorphosis. From the crucible of conflict emerged not just a welfare state and reconstructed infrastructure, but a society founded on the bedrock of equality, social justice, and progress. As the 1950s yielded to the promise of a new era, England stood rejuvenated, a testament to the indomitable spirit of its people who, against the backdrop of adversity, had turned the page to inscribe a narrative of resurgence and renewal.

IMPORTANT PEOPLE, PLACES AND EVENTS DURING THIS PERIOD

PEOPLE:

Clement Attlee: Prime Minister of the United Kingdom from 1945 to 1951, played a key role in the post-war reconstruction and the establishment of the welfare state.

Aneurin Bevan: Minister of Health in Attlee's government and a driving force behind the creation of the National Health Service (NHS) in 1948.

Ernest Bevin: Foreign Secretary during the post-war period, instrumental in shaping England's foreign policy and participating in international collaborations.

The Windrush Generation: Caribbean immigrants who arrived in England between 1948 and 1971, contributing significantly to the cultural diversity of the nation.

Sir Winston Churchill: While not in power during much of the reconstruction era, Churchill's influence and speeches continued to resonate, and he returned as Prime Minister in the 1950s.

PLACES:

National Health Service (NHS): Established in 1948, providing universal healthcare and becoming a cornerstone of the welfare state.

Council Estates and Post-war Suburbs: Significant urban developments aimed at addressing the housing crisis, reshaping the landscape of cities.

The Festival of Britain (1951): A nationwide celebration showcasing technological and cultural achievements, promoting a sense of national pride.

The Open University (Established in 1969): Contributed to the democratisation of education by providing accessible higher education to a broader population.

EVENTS:

End of World War II (1945): Marked the beginning of the post-war reconstruction era, with England facing the immense task of rebuilding after the devastating war.

Housing Acts of 1946 and 1957: Legislation aimed at addressing the housing shortage by promoting the construction of new homes and communities.

The Swinging Sixties (Late 1950s to 1960s): A cultural revolution characterised by vibrant youth culture, fashion, and music.

Marshall Plan (1948–1951): A significant international collaboration providing financial aid to European countries, including England, for post-war reconstruction.

1951 General Election: Labour Party's victory solidified the continuation of post-war policies and reforms initiated by Clement Attlee's government.

CHAPTER 14 - COLD WAR ERA

1950-1991 A.D.

England now found itself at the heart of a new global struggle—the Cold War. The geopolitical landscape was reshaped by the ideological confrontation between the Western and Eastern blocs, and England, emerging from the ravages of conflict, had to navigate the intricate dance between these opposing forces.

The Formation of NATO in 1948

The post-war period witnessed a realignment of alliances. England, once united with the Soviet Union against the Axis powers, saw the dissolution of this wartime coalition. The ideological divide solidified, and England unequivocally aligned itself with the Western bloc. This commitment was underscored by the formation of the North Atlantic Treaty Organisation (NATO) in 1949, a strategic alliance intended to counterbalance the perceived threat of communism.

As the echoes of World War II still reverberated, England found itself drawn into the Korean War. Responding to the call of the United Nations, England became entangled in a distant conflict, supporting South Korea against the communist forces from the North. The war, a proxy confrontation in the overarching Cold War narrative, highlighted England's global engagements and the complex geopolitical realities of the time.

The Suez Crisis of 1956 emerged as a defining moment for England. Alongside France and Israel, England sought to assert control over the Suez Canal—a critical waterway. However, the crisis laid bare the diminishing influence of colonial powers in the post-war era. It marked a turning point, signalling the decline of the old imperial order in the face of evolving global dynamics.

The Cuban Missile Crisis of 1962 brought the world to the brink of nuclear conflict. England, in steadfast unity with its Western allies, closely monitored the perilous standoff between the United States and the Soviet Union. The crisis underscored the global ramifications of the Cold War, as ideologies clashed on the geopolitical stage.

In sport, England hosted the FIFA World Cup in 1966, and it proved to be a historic tournament for the host nation. The final, held at Wembley Stadium on July 30, 1966, saw England face West Germany. The match ended 2-2 in regular time, with

Geoff Hurst scoring a hat-trick in extra time to secure a 4-2 victory for England.

The latter part of the 1960s and the 1970s marked a period of de-escalation and détente in international relations. England, deftly navigating the nuances of this evolving landscape, cautiously embraced a thaw in its dealings with the Soviet Union. Notably, agreements like SALT I were emblematic of concerted efforts to manage the arms race, hinting at the prospect of a more cooperative and collaborative future. During this era, diplomatic overtures and negotiations played a crucial role in fostering a climate of increased understanding and reduced tension between England and the Soviet Union, reflecting a shared commitment to peaceful coexistence amid the complexities of global geopolitics.

The Thatcher era, spanning from 1979 to 1990, witnessed a resolute stand against the perceived Soviet threat. Prime Minister Margaret Thatcher, aligned with President Reagan administration's assertive anti-Soviet stance, actively participated in NATO policies aimed at countering Soviet influence in Europe. The era was marked by a steadfast opposition to the Eastern bloc and a commitment to preserving Western values.

The Falklands War, which occurred in 1982 between Argentina and the United Kingdom, was a conflict over the sovereignty of the Falkland Islands, a remote British Overseas Territory in the South Atlantic. Tensions had been escalating for years, and in April 1982, Argentine forces invaded the islands. The UK swiftly responded by dispatching a task force to reclaim the territories. The conflict lasted for 10 weeks, resulting in the liberation of the Falklands by British forces in June 1982. The war had significant geopolitical implications and had lasting effects on both Argentina and the UK. It remains a pivotal event in modern military history.

Ronald Reagan and Margaret Thatcher

The late 1980s witnessed the culmination of the Cold War, as symbolised by the fall of the Berlin Wall in 1989 and the subsequent dissolution of the Soviet Union in 1991. These momentous events reshaped the geopolitical landscape on a global scale. England, an observer to these seismic shifts, confronted the challenge of adapting to a new era — a time defined by the definitive conclusion of the Cold War. The geopolitical transformations of this period prompted England to reassess its diplomatic strategies and navigate the complexities of a post-Cold War world, where the dynamics of international relations underwent profound changes.

In retrospect, England's journey through the Cold War was an intricate event of diplomacy, tensions, and transformation. The geopolitical complexities of the time tested the nation's resilience and adaptability, ultimately shaping England into a transformed entity as it emerged from the crucible of history.

IMPORTANT PEOPLE, PLACES AND EVENTS DURING THIS PERIOD

PEOPLE:

Winston Churchill: The iconic British Prime Minister during World War II, his role extended into the early years of the Cold War.

Clement Attlee: Succeeded Churchill as Prime Minister and played a crucial role in establishing the post-war welfare state.

Margaret Thatcher: The "Iron Lady," she became Prime Minister in 1979 and was a key figure during the latter part of the Cold War.

Harold Wilson: Led the Labour Party and served as Prime Minister during two non-consecutive terms in the 1960s and 1970s.

PLACES:

London: The capital city, which housed key government and intelligence agencies actively involved in Cold War strategies.

Cambridge: The university town where the infamous Cambridge Spy Ring, a group of British spies, operated during the Cold War.

Greenham Common: Site of protests against the deployment of American nuclear missiles in the 1980s.

EVENTS:

The Berlin Airlift (1948-1949): England played a crucial role in supplying West Berlin during the Soviet blockade.

Korean War (1950-1953): England participated in the UN forces against North Korea, marking its involvement in early Cold War conflicts.

Cuban Missile Crisis (1962): Though not directly involved, England was a key ally of the United States during this tense standoff with the Soviet Union.

The Falklands War (1982): A brief but intense conflict between Argentina and the United Kingdom over the sovereignty of the Falkland Islands that saw British forces successfully reclaim the territories.

Fall of the Berlin Wall (1989): Symbolic of the end of the Cold War, this event marked the reunification of East and West Germany.

CHAPTER 15 - MODERN ENGLAND

1991-PRESENT

The turning of the Cold War's final pages ushered England into a chapter defined by globalisation, economic undulations, political transformations, and an unyielding quest to delineate its identity in an ever-evolving world. The period from 1991 to the present unfurls as a saga intricate in its nuances, marked by resilience, adaptation, and an unremitting exploration of England's role in the modern era.

With the echoes of the Cold War fading, England entered an era shaped by the dissolution of the Soviet Union. Globalisation became the clarion call, and London, the beating heart of the nation, transformed into a cosmopolitan hub. Its skyline, adorned with architectural marvels, symbolised England's readiness to engage with the world in an expansive dance of ideas, trade, and cultural exchange.

The late 20th and early 21st centuries posed formidable economic challenges, testing England's economic mettle. The reverberations of the global financial crisis of 2008 echoed through the nation, triggering debates on fiscal policies and social welfare. Austerity measures were implemented, yet England showcased resilience, adapting to economic shifts, and fostering innovation across sectors ranging from technology to finance.

The political landscape underwent a metamorphosis during this period. The New Labour era, spearheaded by Prime Minister Tony Blair, unfolded policies mirroring the zeitgeist of a changing society. Simultaneously, constitutional shifts saw powers devolving to Scotland, Wales, and Northern Ireland, redefining the contours of governance. The resurgence of English nationalism prompted soul-searching on autonomy and identity within the broader British framework.

Amidst the political and economic flux, England's cultural landscape experienced a renaissance. The nation continued to be a lodestar in the global cultural firmament, with literature, music, and the arts flourishing. Celebrating its diversity, England acknowledged the myriad contributions of communities from varied backgrounds. The Windrush generation's impact endured, and multiculturalism became a defining aspect of the national identity.

Multicultural England

Advancements in technology marked a seismic shift, propelling England into the digital age. The rise of the internet, the establishment of Silicon Roundabout in London, and strides in scientific research positioned the nation at the forefront of technological innovation. England embraced the digital revolution, transforming not only its economic landscape but also the very fabric of daily life.

The modern era proved to be a crucible for profound social transformations and challenges in the United Kingdom. Discussions surrounding equality, LGBTQ+ rights, and environmental sustainability gained increased prominence, reflecting the evolving societal landscape. In the realm of social justice, England actively engaged in dialogues aimed at fostering inclusivity, addressing pertinent issues that touched the lives of its diverse populace.

The seismic decision to depart from the European Union, commonly known as Brexit, not only ignited fervent political and economic debates but also spurred introspection on the nation's identity and its position in the global narrative. This monumental event in 2016 marked a pivotal crossroads, prompting contemplation on themes of sovereignty, trade agreements, and England's trajectory on the world stage.

Amidst navigating the complexities of a global terrain, England faced multifaceted challenges encompassing terrorism, climate change, and the refugee crisis. Demonstrating a commitment to humanitarian causes, the nation actively participated in international collaborations, solidifying its role in the broader global community. These endeavours underscored England's acknowledgment of its responsibilities on the world stage.

As the repercussions of Brexit continued to unfold, they reshaped the political dynamics of the nation, triggering a recalibration of England's standing in the international arena. The ongoing dialogue on these transformative events underscores the resilience and adaptability of a nation navigating the intricate mixture of global affairs.

A 'YES' Vote for Brexit in 2016

The COVID-19 pandemic, starting in 2019, profoundly impacted England. The government, led by Prime Minister Boris Johnson, implemented strict lockdown measures to curb the spread of the virus and alleviate pressure on the NHS. Vaccination campaigns played a pivotal role in the response. The public endured economic and social challenges, with businesses closing and job losses. Nevertheless, communities rallied together, fostering a sense of solidarity. As the vaccination rollout gained momentum, restrictions were gradually eased, marking a transition to a post-pandemic era. The experience underscored the importance of preparedness and collective action in addressing global challenges.

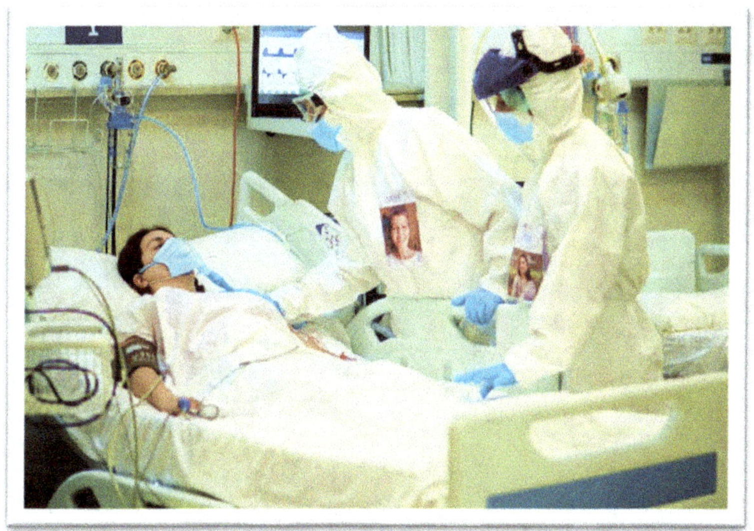

COVID-19 Hit England Severely

On 8th September 2022, England and the entire United Kingdom experienced a profound moment in its history as Queen Elizabeth II passed away after an extraordinary reign spanning 70 years and 214 days. The news of her demise marked the end of an era, and the nation mourned the loss of a revered monarch.

Queen Elizabeth II's reign was characterised by stability, continuity, and significant social change. During her long and impactful tenure, she witnessed the transformation of the world and played a central role in adapting the monarchy to the challenges of the modern era.

The embellishments of this moment lie in the legacy left behind by Queen Elizabeth II – a legacy of dedication to public service, a commitment to duty, and an unwavering sense of continuity. As the nation reflected on her reign, tributes flowed in from all corners, acknowledging the Queen's role as a symbol of continuity and stability.

Queen Elizabeth II in 2015

In the wake of her passing, the country entered a period of mourning, with events and ceremonies honouring her life and contributions. The transition to a new era, marked by the succession of the throne, added a layer of significance to this moment in England's contemporary history.

Upon the passing of Queen Elizabeth II. Charles, the Prince of Wales, ascended to the throne as King Charles III. The transition marked a historic moment in England's contemporary history.

King Charles III and Queen Camilla (Coronation Day)

As the new monarch, King Charles III faced the responsibility of continuing the traditions and adapting to the challenges of the modern era. The nation witnessed ceremonies and events commemorating the transition, reflecting on the legacy of the previous monarch and anticipating the direction of the new reign.

The current Prime Minister of the United Kingdom is Rishi Sunak. He assumed office on October 25, 2022, succeeding Liz Truss. Sunak is the first British Asian and Hindu to hold the office of Prime Minister in the UK.

As the modern era unfolded, England's narrative became a story of adaptation, resilience, and an unyielding quest to define its identity amidst the complexities of the contemporary world. This ongoing saga of tradition, progress, and an unwavering spirit, stands as a testament to the nation's ability to navigate the currents of the 21st century. The pages of this chapter continue to be written, each moment adding another layer to England's unfolding chapters.

IMPORTANT PEOPLE, PLACES AND EVENTS DURING THIS PERIOD

PEOPLE:

Tony Blair: Elected as Prime Minister in 1997, Blair's New Labour government marked a shift in British politics.

Gordon Brown: Succeeded Blair as Prime Minister in 2007 and dealt with economic challenges during the global financial crisis.

David Cameron: Leader of the Conservative Party, he became Prime Minister in 2010, leading a coalition government.

Theresa May: Took office as Prime Minister in 2016, dealing with the aftermath of the Brexit referendum.

Boris Johnson: Prime Minister, known for his role in the Brexit campaign.

PLACES:

London: Continues to be a global financial hub, with ongoing urban development and cultural significance.

EVENTS:

Good Friday Agreement (1998): Marked a significant step towards peace in Northern Ireland, bringing an end to the Troubles.

2005 London Bombings: Coordinated terrorist attacks on public transport in London, causing significant loss of life and injuries.

Financial Crisis (2008): England, like many other countries, faced economic challenges during the global financial downturn.

Brexit Referendum (2016): The UK voted to leave the European Union, leading to significant political and economic consequences.

COVID-19 Pandemic (2019): England, along with the rest of the world, has been dealing with the challenges posed by the ongoing global pandemic.

Important Rulers of England

Alfred the Great (871–899): Alfred was the King of Wessex and is often considered the first King of England. He successfully defended England against Viking invasions and implemented legal reforms.

William the Conqueror (1066–1087): William, Duke of Normandy, defeated King Harold II at the Battle of Hastings in 1066. He became the first Norman King of England, marking the Norman Conquest.

Henry II (1154–1189): Henry was the first of the Plantagenet kings. He strengthened royal authority, established common law, and had conflicts with Thomas Becket.

Richard the Lionheart (1189–1199): Known for his role in the Third Crusade. Richard spent little time in England during his reign and was captured on his way back from the Holy Land.

King John (1199–1216): John faced challenges such as conflict with the barons, leading to the sealing of the Magna Carta in 1215.

Edward I (1272–1307): Known for his military campaigns in Wales and Scotland. Referred to as the "Hammer of the Scots."

Henry VIII (1509–1547): Notable for his six marriages and the English Reformation. Established the Church of England after breaking with the Catholic Church.

Elizabeth I (1558–1603): The last Tudor monarch. Known for her long and prosperous reign, the defeat of the Spanish Armada, and the flourishing of the arts.

Oliver Cromwell (1653–1658): Lord Protector during the Interregnum after the English Civil War. Ruled as a de facto head of state.

Charles II (1660–1685): Restored the monarchy after the Interregnum. Known for his Merry Monarch reign, marked by a more relaxed atmosphere compared to the Puritan era.

Queen Victoria (1837–1901): The longest-reigning monarch in British history. The Victorian era saw significant social, economic, and technological changes.

Elizabeth II (1952-2023): Has witnessed significant changes in the British Empire, its transformation into the Commonwealth, and modern global developments.

King Charles III (2023- to date): The former Prince of Wales and current reigning monarch.

LITERATURE:

Geoffrey Chaucer (c. 1343–1400):

- Often referred to as the "Father of English Literature."

- Best known for "The Canterbury Tales," a collection of stories written in Middle English.

William Shakespeare (1564–1616):

- Regarded as one of the greatest playwrights and poets in the English language.

- Works include plays like "Romeo and Juliet," "Hamlet," and "Macbeth."

Jane Austen (1775–1817):

- Renowned for her novels exploring the social commentary of the British landed gentry.

- Works include "Pride and Prejudice" and "Sense and Sensibility."

Charles Dickens (1812–1870):

- A prolific Victorian novelist and social critic.

- Notable works include "A Tale of Two Cities," "Oliver Twist," and "Great Expectations."

SCIENCE:

Isaac Newton (1643–1727):

- Mathematician and physicist.

- Formulated the laws of motion and universal gravitation.

Charles Darwin (1809–1882):

- Naturalist who developed the theory of evolution by natural selection.

- Author of "On the Origin of Species."

Ada Lovelace (1815–1852):

- Mathematician and writer, often regarded as the world's first computer programmer.

- Collaborated with Charles Babbage on his mechanical general-purpose computer, the Analytical Engine.

POLITICS:

Winston Churchill (1874–1965):

- Prime Minister during crucial periods of World War II.

- Known for his powerful speeches and leadership.

Emmeline Pankhurst (1858–1928):

- Suffragette leader campaigning for women's right to vote.

- Founder of the Women's Social and Political Union.

Clement Attlee (1883–1967):

- Prime Minister after World War II.

- Implemented significant social reforms, including the establishment of the National Health Service (NHS).

MUSIC:

William Byrd (c. 1540–1623):

- Renowned composer and organist in the Renaissance period.

- Known for his contributions to English sacred music.

The Beatles (formed in 1960):

- Iconic rock band with members John Lennon, Paul McCartney, George Harrison, and Ringo Starr.

- Revolutionised popular music and culture.

EXPLORATION:

Captain James Cook (1728–1779):

- Explorer, navigator, and cartographer.

- Made significant voyages, including the first European contact with the eastern coastline of Australia.

Ernest Shackleton (1874–1922):

- Antarctic explorer.

- Led the Endurance expedition and is known for his remarkable leadership during a disastrous Antarctic expedition.

These influential individuals have left a lasting impact on various aspects of English history, contributing to literature, science, politics, music, and exploration.

A Timeline of English Sporting Glory

1882: The Ashes Series Begins: The historic Ashes series commenced with a notable cricket match at The Oval, where England faced defeat against Australia, leading to the creation of the iconic Ashes urn.

1924: Harold Abrahams' Olympic Gold: Harold Abrahams, the sprinter immortalised in the film "Chariots of Fire," clinched the gold medal in the 100 metres at the 1924 Paris Olympics, showcasing English excellence in athletics.

1930s: Fred Perry's Tennis Achievements: Fred Perry, a tennis legend, achieved remarkable success in the 1930s, securing multiple Grand Slam singles titles and becoming the last English player to do so before the era of Andy Murray.

1930s: Sir Henry Cotton's Golfing Dominance: Sir Henry Cotton made a significant impact on golf in the 1930s, securing three Open Championships and solidifying his place as one of England's greatest golfers.

1940s-1950s: Reg Harris in Cycling: Reg Harris, a prominent cyclist, dominated the cycling scene in the post-war era, winning multiple world championships and Olympic medals.

1953: Sir Stanley Matthews' FA Cup Final Performance: Sir Stanley Matthews delivered a memorable performance in the 1953 FA Cup final, helping Blackpool come from behind to win against Bolton Wanderers.

1965: Tom Simpson's Cycling Achievements: Tom Simpson made history in cycling by becoming the first Englishman to wear the yellow jersey in the Tour de France and winning the World Road Race Championship in 1965.

1966: England Wins the FIFA World Cup: The pinnacle of English football history, the national team, led by Sir Alf Ramsey and captained by Bobby Moore, secured victory in the 1966 FIFA World Cup, defeating West Germany in the final at Wembley Stadium.

1980, 1984: Daley Thompson's Decathlon Gold Medals: Daley Thompson showcased his athletic prowess by winning consecutive gold medals in the decathlon at the 1980 Moscow and 1984 Los Angeles Olympics.

1990s: Sir Nick Faldo's Golfing Legacy: Sir Nick Faldo, one of the most successful English golfers, achieved greatness in the 1990s, winning multiple Major championships, including three Masters and three Open Championships.

2003: Jonny Wilkinson's Rugby World Cup Moment: Jonny Wilkinson's dramatic last-minute drop goal in the 2003 Rugby World Cup final secured England's victory against Australia in Sydney, marking a historic moment in rugby history.

2012: Jessica Ennis-Hill's Heptathlon Gold: Jessica Ennis-Hill captured the nation's heart by winning the heptathlon gold at the 2012 London Olympics, showcasing her versatility in track and field.

2012, 2016: Sir Mo Farah's "Double-Double": Sir Mo Farah achieved a rare feat by winning gold in both the 5,000m and 10,000m at both the 2012 London and 2016 Rio Olympics, establishing himself as a long-distance running legend.

2012: Bradley Wiggins' Tour de France Win: Sir Bradley Wiggins made history by becoming the first English cyclist to win the Tour de France in 2012, an achievement that further elevated the status of English cycling.

2013-present: Lewis Hamilton's Formula 1 Dominance: Lewis Hamilton has been a dominant force in Formula 1, consistently winning championships and breaking records, making him one of the most successful English racing drivers in history.

INDEX

S

T

U

V

W

IMAGE CREDITS

Picture Title	Credit Attributions
Royal Arms of England	Public domain, via Wikimedia Commons
The Flag of England	Nicholas Shanks, Public domain, via Wikimedia Commons
The Location of England	Elevatorrailfan, via Wikimedia Commons
Stonehenge c.3000–2500 B.C.	Gareth Wiscombe, via Wikimedia Commons
Early Bronze Age Dagger	Ario1234, via Wikimedia Commons
Cadbury Castle a Bronze/Iron Age Hillfort	Joe D, modified by Jim Champion, via Wikimedia Commons
Maiden Castle Hillfort in Dorset	George Allen (1891–1940), Public domain, via Wikimedia Commons
Watling Street Route	Neddy Seagoon, via Wikimedia Commons
Hadrian's Wall	Fruitsmaak, Public domain, via Wikimedia Commons
Roman Baths in Bath	Diliff, via Wikimedia Commons
Æthelstan, The First King of England	Matthew Paris, Public domain, via Wikimedia Commons
Harald Hardrada in Kirkwall Cathedral	Colin Smith, via wikipedia
Battle of Hastings (Bayeux Tapestry)	Myrabella, Public domain, via Wikimedia Commons
A Page from the Doomsday Book Manuscripts	Percy Benzie Abery, via Wikimedia Commons
Battle of Tewkesbury 1471	Joseph Martin Kronheim, Public domain, via Wikimedia Commons
Portrait of King Henry VII	National Portrait Gallery, Public domain, via Wikimedia Commons
The Family of King Henry VIII	Public domain, via Wikimedia Commons
William Shakespeare	John Taylor, Public domain, via Wikimedia Commons
Sir Walter Raleigh	Public domain, via Wikimedia Commons
The Execution of King Charles I	Public domain, via Wikimedia Commons
The Bill of Rights Ratified at the Revolution by King William, and Queen Mary	Samuel Wale, Public domain, via Wikimedia Commons
Queen Anne	John Closterman, Public domain, via Wikimedia Commons
Mechanised Looms During the Industrial Revolution	Engraver J. Tingle, Public domain, via Wikimedia Commons
British Napoleonic Infantry	Richard Simkin, Public domain, via Wikimedia Commons
The Opening of The Great Exhibition, 1st May 1851	Eugène Lami, Public domain, via Wikimedia Commons
Queen Victoria and Prince Albert	John Jabez Edwin Mayal, Public domain, via Wikimedia Commons
King Edward VII in His Coronation Robes	Luke Fildes, Public domain, via Wikimedia Commons
The Titanic Sailing out of Southampton	Anonymous, Public domain, via Wikimedia Commons
The Arrest of Suffragette Emmeline Pankhurst	Spaarnestad Photo, Public domain, via Wikimedia Commons
World War I Trench Warfare in Somme 1916	John Warwick Brooke, Public domain, via Wikimedia Commons
The German-Soviet Invasion of Poland 1939	Press Agency photographer, Public domain, via Wikimedia Commons
Spitfire and Hurricane from The Battle of Britain	Cpl Gary Morgan MOD, via Wikimedia Commons
London's St Paul's Cathedral after The Blitz	H.Mason, Public domain, via Wikimedia Commons
The First Day of the National Health Service in 1948	Faculty of Health & Life Sciences from Liverpool, UK, via Wikimedia Commons
Festival of Britain Tapestry Souvenir 1951	LondonHistoryatHome, via Wikimedia Commons
The Windrush Generation in the 1950s	www.winnmediaskn.com
The Formation of NATO in 1948	brewminate.com
Ronald Reagan and Margaret Thatcher	Unknown photographer, Public domain, via Wikimedia Commons
Multicultural England	www.paddysletterfromlondon.blogspot.com
A 'YES' Vote for Brexit in 2016	ChiralJon, via Wikimedia Commons
COVID-19 Hit England Severely	www.nih.govnews
Queen Elizabeth II in 2015	PolizeiBerlin, via Wikimedia Commons
King Charles III and Queen Camilla (Coronation Day)	www.people.com

About the Author

Martin Miller-Yianni, a London native born in 1958, initially set forth on the path of a primary school teacher. However, in a remarkable departure from convention in 2005, he chose to explore the enchanting landscapes of Southeastern Europe. It was amidst the rich mixture of diverse lifestyles and cultures in the region that he discovered a newfound passion for writing.

Immersing himself in the role of a journalist and researcher for a highly regarded website dedicated to Southeastern Europe, Martin cultivated a profound understanding of the area. His personal and professional standing through the region became the fertile ground for his creative endeavours. This journey of exploration and insight served as the muse for his latest publication, 'England Through the Ages: A Concise Guide.'

This literary work was a deviation from the norm and not just a product of Martin's personal fascination with his former homeland; rather, it emerged as a response to the curiosity of non-English acquaintances. They sought a comprehensive guide to England, the land of his upbringing and education, showcasing the unique blend of historical richness and contemporary nuances that define the country. In 'England Through the Ages,' Martin eloquently weaves together the threads of history, culture, and personal anecdotes, offering readers a captivating narrative that transcends geographical boundaries.

Other Books by the Author

365 Bulgarian Adventures (2006)
Publication Pending

26 Tales of Humanities Trials
(2023)
ISBN
978-619-92494-8-2

Simple Treasures in Bulgaria
(2008)
ISBN
978-0-9559-8490-7

I'm Bad at Poems
(2022)
ISBN
978-619-92494-2-0

Bulgaria Through the Ages
(2023)
ISBN
978-1-4476-2777-7

Redemption of Love
(2023)
ISBN
978-619-92494-0-6

100 Essential Recipes from Bulgaria
(2011)
ISBN
978-1-4477-0260-3

Romania Through the Ages
(2023)
ISBN
978-619-7742-19-0

North Macedonia Through the Ages
(2023)
ISBN
978-619-7742-25-1

Cyprus Through the Ages
(2023)
ISBN
978-619-7742-22-0

www.ingramcontent.com/pod-product-compliance
Lightning Source LLC
LaVergne TN
LVHW020028170826
845678LV00001B/157

* 9 7 8 6 1 9 7 7 4 2 3 1 2 *